The Zen of Hype

The Zen of Hype

An Insider's Guide to the Publicity Game

Raleigh Pinskey

A Citadel Press Book
Published by Carol Publishing Group

A Citadel Press Book
Published by Carol Publishing Group
Citadel Press is a registered trademark of Carol Communications, Inc.
Editorial Offices: 600 Madison Avenue, New York, N.Y. 10022
Sales & Distribution Offices: 120 Enterprise Avenue, Secaucus, N.J. 07094
In Canada: Musson Book Company, a division of General Publishing Company,
    Ltd., Don Mills, Ontario M3B 2T6

Queries regarding rights and permissions should be addressed to Carol
Publishing Group, 600 Madison Avenue, New York, N.Y. 10022

Carol Publishing Group books are available at special discounts for bulk
purchases, for sales promotions, fund raising, or educational purposes.
Special editions can be created to specifications. For details, contact:
Special Sales Department, Carol Publishing Group, 120 Enterprise Avenue,
Secaucus, N.J. 07094

Manufactured in the United States of America
10   9   8   7   6   5   4   3   2   1

Library of Congress Cataloging-in-Publication Data

Pinskey, Raleigh.
    The zen of hype : an insider's guide to the publicity game / by
Raleigh Pinskey.
        p.   cm.
    "A Citadel Press book."
    ISBN 0–8065–1239–3
    1. Public relations.   2. Publicity.   I. Title.
HD59.P527   1991
659—dc20   91–38822
                                                    CIP

Contents

Acknowledgments   vii

Introduction   3

1. Public Relations vs. Advertising   7

2. The Art of Public Relations   14

3. How to Make Yourself Media Friendly   28

4. How to Get the Media to Cover Your Event   44

5. How to Plan Your Media Campaign   59

6. The Media Kit   65

7. Mailing Lists, the Backbone of Public Relations   74

8. Pitching Your Project to the Media   100

9. Using Gimmicks to Assist Your Pitch   117

10. The Art of Follow-Up   121

11. Interviews   139

12. Wrapping Up the Campaign   150

13. Don't Be Caught Unaware   156

Appendix   167

Acknowledgments

My thanks to my mother, my father, and my brother. Also my thanks to all those in the media and the publicity world and my friends who were kind enough to spend time with me to make this book happen: Diane Abrams, Jonathan Alter, Rebecca Batties, Sunny Bernstein, Gene Busnar, Rosemary Carroll, Eileen Daspin, Mitchell Davis, Dick Delson, Angela Dodson, Jim Dolce, Fern Edison, Brian Enright, Audrey Franklin, Art Garcia, Gale Gardner, Robert Gardner, Don Garrett, Michael Gelman, Dick Gersh, Jane Gilman, David Goggin, Marianne Goldstein, Tom Green, Lyle Gregory, Barry Greenberg, Brian Griffith, Jeff Herman, Dan Hutson, Erik Himmelsbach, Mike Hughes, Jessica Josell, Rick Joyce, Stuart Krasnow, Steve Kritsick, Shelia Peterson-Lowary, Brad LeMack, Bob Levitan, Brian Lewis, Mary Lyons, Michael McKenzie, Terri Mandell, Jim Mandell, Rhonda Markowitz, Randy Matin, Jamie Masada, Frank Meyer, Julian Meyers, Noel Michon, Nan Miller, Andy Muson, Barbara Nachman, Julie Nathanson, Patty Neger, B. L. Ochman, Denise Osso, Pat Phillips, Randy Poe, Jack Popejoy, Frank Radice, Darcy Randall, F. Ribble, Roger Richmond, Liz Rittersporn, Victoria Rose, Kerry Schaffer, Andrew Scher, Flo Selfman, Joe Serling, Bruce Shostak, Les Sinclair, Joshua Simons, Joanne Smale, Richard D. Smith, Alan Steinberg, Debby Supnick, THEO, Bill Thornton, Steve Trager, Dee Vyne, Chris Walker, Dotty Walters, Mickey Wallach, Lance Webster, Paulette Weiss, Dee Westlund, Jennifer Westlund, Michael Wiese, Irwin Zucker.

I would also like to thank the following companies for their cooperation: American Passage Media Services, Audio TV

Features, Bacon's Clipping Service and Media Information Systems, Billboard Publications Media Services, R. R. Bowker, Broadcast Interview Source, Burrelle's Clipping and Media Services, Gale Research, Contacts Newsletter, Derus Media, Morgan-Rand Directory Services, Luce Clipping Service, Metro Publicity Services, National Forensic Services, News USA Inc., North American Precis Syndicate, Media Distribution Services, Para Publishing, Partyline, PR Newswire, Public Relations Society of America, Publicity Express, Radio TV Report, Speak and Grow Rich, Standard Rate and Data Services, Goodphone Communications, Video Monitoring Service.

The Zen of Hype

Introduction
On the Zen of Hype

"Hype is getting someone excited enough to get off his duff and do something."
—Joshua Simons, Events and Sponsorship Marketing Specialist

The word *hype* is slang, believed to have its origins in the Latin word *hyperbole* (from the Greek *huperbolē-*), a combination of *hyper-*, meaning "over," usually implying excess or exaggeration, and *-bole*, meaning "throw." Throwing exaggeration. *Hyperbole* is defined by *Webster's* as "obvious and intentional exaggeration" or as "extravagant statement." *Roget's Thesaurus of Synonyms and Antonyms* lists *hyperbole* under the noun *exaggeration*, making it synonymous with *stretch, high coloring, magnify, expand, go to great lengths, spin a long yarn, misrepresent, puff, boast, bombastic, preposterous,* and *high-flying*.

Quite a family. To me, hype is a positive word when used in the proper context. Positive hype is used daily by the business, financial, and entertainment worlds to generate or increase sales, build a new image or massage a tired one, gain visibility, heighten political awareness, raise funds for charities or a new football field for one's alma mater.

Hype is used to promote one's position, one's ego, one's financial status. It is the taking of something and making it sound like something bigger and more credible. When used to promote and not pummel, when it is positive and not harmful, hype has the ability to bring joy, laughter, celebration, comfort, and riches to those whom it targets.

This book is a firsthand approach to the subject of hype and how it should and should not be practiced. The information is the product of my twelve years as public relations consultant to those in the worlds of products, advertising, and entertainment.

It has always been my contention that once you understand the areas of conflict and common ground between the players, then you will have the foundation to develop the skills and techniques that underlie your success.

This book, therefore, is for those who have attempted to list their PTA "Summertime Fun Fair" on the community radio calendar only to find out later that because they didn't include the proper information, their listing wasn't included.

It is for the inventor who is told by his manufacturer that if he would appear on the national and regional talk shows he could generate many orders, but who, not knowing where to go or what to say, doesn't even try.

It is for those of you who might actually have gotten up the courage to call the newspaper listings and reached the right person, but instead of receiving a pleasant hello, heard *"deadline"* screamed into your ear, followed by a disconnect. Startled and embarrassed, you never called back, and your event never got listed.

It is for the physician who has a substantiated theory pertaining to childhood allergies that she would like to share with the mothers of the world but, because she is not published, thinks she has no way of being heard.

It is for the owner of a new Bed & Bath shop who is told by a newspaper's receptionist that they don't run that kind of item and that he should run an advertisement instead. Trusting the receptionist as the final word on editorial copy, he never again approaches the paper with a story idea.

It is for the civic group that wants to take an underground issue public but decides not to call the local television news for fear of bothering them, because the idea is something so obscure that they would not be interested. And so the group loses the issue in the election because they aren't able to get enough support.

It is for you, the person who deserves mention in a series the paper is doing on local businesspeople. Because you didn't know who or what to ask for, you got the runaround and quit out of frustration.

This book is for all of you. It will show you how to tell the world about yourself, how to hype yourself, your business, your client, even your dog who does crazy pet tricks. It will show you how to take anything and, by the very act of bringing it to the attention of the public, enhance it. This book has been written to help you achieve your objectives, to arm you with all the tools and inside information that are currently available only to professionals and to people who can afford to hire publicists, so that you too can increase sales, raise awareness, and bring attention to yourself to further your goals.

But this book doesn't take the "Simon Says" approach you might find in other books on the subject. Rather than telling you only what I know about how to write a media release or how to make a follow-up phone call, I have supplemented my own expertise by interviewing hundreds of top media professionals in television, radio, and print and asking them how they want or don't want a media release written and whether they want to receive a follow-up phone call. I asked over one hundred editors, producers, bookers, assignment editors, and photo editors about their pet peeves, likes, dislikes, and opinions on a wide range of day-to-day interactions with the public relations community. I wanted to know how these interactions affected their decisions and attitudes about covering events and stories. And then I asked those in the "PR" game how they felt about the media, along with how they dealt with the likes, dislikes, and opinions directed to them by those in the media.

- We discussed *to do, to take,* and *to have* lunch—or *not to* at all.
- When and if it is appropriate to send releases by gorillas, balloons, or bunny rabbits.
- We labored over faxing, voice mail, overnight mail, and tightly wrapped packages (which are rated by how many fingernails will bite the dust when opening them).
- How to give and how to take an interview. How to hold an when not to hold a press conference, as well as what kinds of bagels to serve.
- When to spend money and when not to, even when you think you should.

As you go through these chapters underlining, highlighting, and memorizing, please understand that the most important tool is an open mind—an attitude that includes doubt, optimism, and the ability to see things as fresh and new, because no matter what you learn here, and because human beings are on both sides of the conversation, the rules of the game can and will change. This is why I have chosen to title the book *The Zen of Hype.* In Zen, you are shown how you must "stay in the moment" in order to have what you are learning have meaning. Although hype has formulas and structures, each project must be treated as if entirely new. In order to succeed, you must confront each project with the well-honed tools you used in the past, but you do not have to follow the same floor plan. If you take what you have learned from the past and use it as a rigid frame, you cannot create a new environment. View all you will read here as flexible substance. Use the information as tools to assist you in getting what you want accomplished. And, as always, stay in the moment.

1

Public Relations vs. Advertising

"*Caveat emptor.* Let the buyer beware."
—Anonymous

"Step right up, folks, that's right, little lady, and you too, sir, just a little closer. I want you to keep your attention on my right hand at all times. Now, the contents of this little brown bottle I hold in my hand will give you the confidence to speak to anyone, I mean anyone you could imagine. One swallow of this mint-flavored elixir will infuse your system with coded knowledge of the ages. It will give you the guile and cunning of Mata Hari and Lucrezia Borgia with the tempered sensitivity of the Pope and Mother Teresa. Yes, folks, this potion will put the world under your spell so that you can get anyone and anything you want in life. Step right up, that's right, little lady, just a little closer."

Surely you recognize the caricature of the snake-oil salesman? The flimflam man? The carpetbagger? Names for those to beware of—those who deal in the "H" word. Hype, the drug that caters to egos and lines the pockets of those who spew it out.

There are those who feel that the venerated art of the snake-oil salesman has taken up residence in the public relations parlor, home of the media consultant, a.k.a. publicist, a.k.a. press agent, a.k.a. flack. B. L. Ochman takes offense at being thought of as a modern-day flimflam lady. This enterprising president of her own company doesn't think of what she does as hype. She thinks of it as a creative way of getting her client's story told in the media in a favorable light.

So, what we have here is that PR is fine when it is the business of information, but when it is the business of hype, it's a different kind of business. To me, hype means enthusiasm. People will not believe you or believe in your product if you don't hype—if you don't show enthusiasm. But it's how you do it. You have to be enthusiastic without being a caricature. You want to make things big, not just bigger than they are. You want to make people successful. You want to make heroes for those who don't manufacture their own enthusiasm, their own hype.

PR vs. Advertising

When your circus comes to town and you put up a sign, that's advertising.

If you put the sign on the back of an elephant and you march the elephant through town, that's sales promotion.

If the elephant, with the sign still on his back, tramples through the mayor's flower garden and the paper reports it, that's publicity.

If you can get the mayor to laugh about it and forgive the elephant and ride in the circus with no hard feelings, then you've mastered the art of public relations.

The saying goes: "In advertising you pay for it, in PR your pray for it."

Three Basic Ways to Get the Word Out:

1. Advertising, the most expensive method.
2. Direct marketing, the next most expensive method.

3. Public relations, the least expensive, but the most time consuming.

WHY ADVERTISE?

When you advertise, you can choose what you want to say, the day you want it to appear, the size of the type, the artwork that accompanies it, the section in which it will appear, and, in many cases, the page. This is known as control, and in advertising you have it, every step of the way.

WHY DO DIRECT MARKETING?

When you engage in direct marketing, you are able to hone in and target the exact demographics you wish to attract. You have a captive audience, usually one with a history of interest in what you are representing. Direct marketing is also a controlled vehicle, but more targeted than advertising.

WHY DO PR?

In PR you do none of the above The only real control you have is that you can say no. If you don't like the publication or the radio or television show, you can refuse to do the interview. If you don't like the way the line of questioning is going, you can walk out. If you don't like the interviewer, you can request a change or cancel the interview. Otherwise, you are at the mercy of others as to content, presentation, artwork, timing, and page placement.

When you advertise, you hire an absolute—a tangible. When you do PR, you hire an intangible, a dream, an aspiration. If you are prepared to do that, to hope for the chance that you will have your picture and story plastered all over the world, state, city, or your particular industry, then do publicity. If what you want is an absolute, no changes, no chances, no maybes, then advertise.

Why Choose PR Over Advertising

In advertising you have two participants:

1. the client who relates the "story" directly to a representative of the media outlet,
2. the media outlet that relates the original and unchanged "story" to the audience.

In PR you have three participants:

1. the client who relates the information directly to the media,
2. the media,
3. a representative of the media, whose job it is to comment on that information in his own words. This third party is perceived by consumers as someone looking out for their interests, somewhat like a consumer watchdog.

According to *Book Marketing Update*, people are seven times as likely to respond to a third-party article about a product or service as they are to an advertisement. If someone else tries the product, tastes the food, experiences the resort, and then shares an opinion, the consumer outcome is translated into "What can be wrong?" In other words, PR can give you credibility.

Alternatives to Conventional Advertising and PR

If you are not ready to deal with the third party who just might rip your restaurant to shreds, make fun of your lifelong dream, underrate your gallery, or pan your health spa, and if you don't have the money to launch and sustain a conventional advertising campaign, you could go the route of the nineties…and have your cake and eat it too!

Enter the info-mercial and the advitorial. The purpose of these two relatively new kids on the block is to combine the credibility of the third-party endorsement with the mass marketing techniques of advertising.

THE ADVITORIAL

This is the ingenious marriage of advertisement and editorial. You've seen it many times in print media but may not have known it was a "paid advertisement." It looked like third-party-endorsed editorial when in fact a company constructed the image, wrote the copy, bought the placement, and designed the advitorial to look exactly like a third-party editorial. Legally, an advitorial must have a disclaimer identifying it as an advertisement. If you look closely, you will usually find the notice in very small print, off to the side or at the bottom—many readers may miss it as they scan the controlled information.

INFO-MERCIALS

An info-mercial is the marriage of information and commercials and has been on the scene since the seventies. Mobil Oil Corporation produced mini–news reports that had the look and feel of news, except the information and intent were controlled by the company. Remember the old Timex watch commercials and how they had a "newsworthy" sensationalism about them? Both were done with a third-party credibility factor in order to win over the audience. The format hasn't changed.

The Federal Communications Commission (FCC) now defines TV info-mercials as continuous advertising in excess of fifteen minutes. The floodgates for such "programming" were opened when the Reagan administration lifted the amount of time a TV station could use for commercials. Creative minds turned a loophole into a bonanza.

You may have already seen info-mercials and not have known they were paid advertising programming. They, like the advitorial, must display a disclaimer alerting the audience to the fact that they are paid advertisements, but for now, they must only do so at the beginning and end of the program.

An info-mercial's producers take the credible format of a newscast, public information show, talk show, cooking demonstration, or travelogue and weave a story line replete with what seem to be innocent participants providing the audience with third-party opinions. Info-mercials sell everything from vacation spots, memory courses, tooth whiteners, and car polish to time-saving house-painting techniques, diet menu plans, and real estate get-rich-quick techniques. If it can be sold, they will sell it.

TV is not alone in this genre. I have placed my clients on radio talk shows that sold product time. They actually charged the talk show "guests" a fee to promote their project. In other words, they would interview you or your client for a price. The more time exposure you were willing to pay for, the more time you got.

The growth in advitorials and info-mercials has been prompted in part by the decrease in traditional editorial space, as well as the trend in editorial policy toward the new and exciting and a reluctance to redo a story that has been done within a certain time period (usually not less than a year and sometimes up to five years, if a redo is allowed at all).

A magazine might do a Bed and Breakfast story only once a year, and only then revolving around a theme. If your business isn't the "great view of the ocean" or the "yuppy–turned–innkeeper" type place, it probably won't get included in this year's feature on Bed and Breakfasts. If the section that highlights new and interesting products featured a bottle opener in the last six months, it might not include another bottle opener for six months or more. Many lifestyle sections have seasonal editorial calendars and you just have to wait and hope the editorial department will want to include you. And so it is that many industries such as products, vacation spots, health and fitness facilities and methods are looking to "do their thing" by way of the "paid for" method.

Remember that info-mercials and advitorials are pure advertising. With info-mercials, align yourself with a production company whose third-party endorsement is not fake or fabricated. Not uncommonly, the "third party" in many of the info-mercials is hired by the company to appear impartial. Recently, several investigative talk and news shows have gone behind the scenes of the info-mercials and have come up with gruesome stories of unethical manipulation to make the product perform as the text claims. If you choose to get involved with advitorials or info-mercials, make certain that the picture you paint is not brighter than the real thing.

In the long run, honesty will always win out.

2

The Art of Public Relations

"Presidents, kings, and CEOs are not running the world, their PR firms are."
—Lyle Gregory, booker for "The Michael Jackson Show," KABC Talkradio, Los Angeles

When somebody mentions the term *press agent*, do you picture troll-like people with phones attached to their ears, postage stamps stuck to their fingers, and list upon list draping their bodies like a second skin? When you hear the term *flack* do you conjure up a picture of a bent-back curmudgeon wearing a green visor and rolled-up sleeves and smoking a smelly cigar, telling you about the next-best-thing-since-sliced-bread? How about the term *publicist*? Do you think of a handsomely attired gentleman or a stylish woman in a silk suit handing over business cards from an expensive briefcase and jotting notes with a Mont Blanc pen? Do you smile and relax and think of people who over caviar discuss how they intend to glide their clients over troubled waters and through obstacle courses with ease?

People frequently ask me the difference between a press agent, a publicist, and one who does public relations. Basically, there is no difference. Some people surmise that the term *press agent* is old-fashioned and conjures up gossip columnists and ambulance chasers. As for publicists, some conceive of them as "worker bees," the ones who write the releases and place the calls. Those who "do public relations" are considered the cream of the industry, the movers and shakers. They have the fancy offices, the right political connections in an industry, and bankers and lawyers in their court; they are able to get the best table or front-row seats at a moment's notice. But don't let that blind you. Some of the best, most influential, and most respected people in this industry work out of their homes, have one phone with call waiting, and take their meetings at the local eatery.

I polled my colleagues to discover what they thought were good qualities for a PR person. They came up with:

- Creativity and imagination
- Resourcefulness
- Thick skin
- Loyalty
- The ability to keep a secret
- Maternal/paternal instincts
- An understanding and forgiving nature
- Energy and drive
- The eyes of an eagle, the heart of a lamb, and the emotions of a zombie

Besides Contacting the Media, What Does a Publicist Do?

Goes in after female fans who have followed a male client into the men's room;

Smooths things over with the media when the client gets in a bind or makes a mistake;

Flies cross-country to hand-deliver the client's product to a TV talk show so there won't be any possibility of a "no show" because of a shipper's error;

Baby-sits the client's twins so the client can do an interview;

Literally gives the shirt off her back when the client stains hers in the Green Room while waiting to make a TV appearance;

Takes the place of his client in a talk show run-through
    because he is in an important merger meeting;

Helps newly unemployed media contacts find new jobs;

Negotiates the best deal possible for both sides, emerging,
    one hopes, with his and his client's reputation intact and
    bills paid;

Feeds the pets while the client is away on a speaking tour.

Besides the above, our job as publicists is to know what
every editor, talent coordinator, producer, journalist, and
reporter is looking to get for their talk shows, sections,
segments, or columns. Whatever their title, it is our job to
know what they are looking for. We have to come up with
something about a client that is going to interest them and
have a payoff for their audience.

Los Angeles PR man Dick Delson's view is that a PR person
presents a client in the best light so that the client will benefit
financially and with positive recognition. He sees our job as
getting the message out there so that John Q. Public buys it.

New York PR woman B. L. Ochman describes what we do as
"a mail and sales job." We sell ideas—we sell whatever—but
we sell it.

Barry Greenberg, president of Celebrity Connection, sees
us as taking clients that are doing the same thing as everyone
else is doing and making them more visible—not more
special, just more visible, because people perceive you as
being special if you are more visible. If you are also able to put
a unique spin on what it is you do, then people who need to
come up with story ideas will beat a path to your door.

I once saw a plaque in a colleague's office that read:

A PRESS AGENT IS THE FIRST TO BE HIRED,
THE LAST TO BE PAID,
THE FIRST TO BE FIRED,
AND THE LAST TO BE TOLD…ANYTHING,
INCLUDING HE'S BEING FIRED.

So why do we do it? Why do we come to work each day, pick up the phone with crossed fingers, and hope the media will take our call and accept the pitch? Sound terribly masochistic? Well, folks, I can tell you that despite the angst we experience from the media, from clients, from product reps, and the attitude directed to us in general, this job is not so different from one in any other field of endeavor, so relax and enjoy it. It does have many up sides.

Toronto publicist Joanne Smale loves being the person who helps make the client successful. Her reward is satisfaction and a tremendous sense of pride that she helped someone's career to blossom. She loves to see someone bask in the lights that she, as one of the cogs in the wheel, helped illuminate.

Flo Selfman sees herself and public relations as a service business. "I'm not curing cancer, but sometimes the services we contribute help aid the fight."

"The Michael Jackson Show" booker, Lyle Gregory, likes being a part of linking the general public to social and political issues of interest. He likes working every day with upbeat, dedicated, and creative people; knowing stories and information that the public may not be aware of for days to come; moving in a world of excitement, stimulation, and variety with immediate results; and being able to assist the nonprofits and the social activists of the world who don't have a huge budget for fancy promotions by putting them on the air. It gives Lyle a chance to be David fighting Goliath, to be Johnny Appleseed, to be a part of the democratic process.

Who Do the Media Feel Are Good PR People?

Those who are active in the community, and who have a broad view of issues;

Those who know both sides of the game, understand it, and respect it. Those who know what their job is, what our job is, and where the twains meet;

Those who make it their business to know a particular media, with an understanding of what the media is looking for and what we're not;

Those who don't try and snow us with what they know, or try and pull the wool over our eyes;

Those who act with integrity and honesty;

Those who know not to try to flatter us in order to get in our good graces, or who will go behind our back to another level if we decide not to do the story;

Those who won't run through a client laundry list;

Those who don't try to manipulate or treat us as if we were born yesterday and have no conception of what is newsworthy and what isn't;

Someone who does not waste our time with inappropriate requests, does not use superlatives to describe an inconsequential client, and does not think that the client is so close to God that he or she won't do the interview unless we give the client the cover story;

Someone who won't play one media against the other by promising an item or exclusive and giving it instead to another media, or shut out a smaller media when they get a more influential offer;

Someone who knows not to pretend to be our long lost buddy when they call to pitch or to whine when we say no;

Someone who will go overboard to help us get access to their client when something newsworthy happens;

Those who don't take us off their event list when we are between jobs;

Those who understand that the bottom line is to produce the best possible show, magazine, or newspaper;

Someone who understands what we need to make it happen and has it all ready to go;

Those who have taken journalism classes and can distinguish how they want their client to come across and how the media will actually approach the story;

Those who know enough not to send unnecessary updates every week;

Those who recognize the importance of support staff, treat them properly, and use them to their best advantage;

Those who really know how to differentiate between business and friendship.

How to Choose a PR Firm

The 1987 Bureau of Labor Statistics' Census of Service Industries report estimates that there are 5,060 PR firms, with approximately fifty thousand independent and company publicists.

LARGE AGENCIES VS. SMALL AGENCIES

Large and small agencies both have upsides and downsides. For example, not all large agencies are suited to handle accounts that need a great deal of attention, and not all small agencies have the clout to help certain clients, and vice versa.

Large agencies have to maintain a full client roster to cover their enormous overhead. Small agencies, although they want to make money, have more freedom to pick and choose clients who satisfy their creative and ethical needs. Not that the big guys can't be creative, but the amount of time they have to invest in the nurturing process may not be as great.

Many of the large agencies hire people away from the small agencies because the small agencies are a good, thorough, training ground.

Many small agencies are started by responsible and creative people who became frustrated by not being able to provide the clients with the quality time and proper campaign follow-up when they were in a big agency.

In a one-person agency, the person who owns the company is the one actively working on the accounts. The addition of one or two account executives usually does not hinder the quality of the work if the one whose name is on the door is an everyday, hands-on, integral part of the office. But you must establish this when making the decision. Believe the chief, but most importantly, talk to the Indians. Find out how the agency works, or rather, who in the agency is responsible for the actual work, before you make your decision to sign on as a client. If there is only one person, the owner, ask to see the client roster and call the clients for their point of view. If there are employees, ask them who really does the work. Don't be afraid to ask around. It's your money, your good name, and your career.

Small agencies represent themselves on the premise of individual attention. Large agencies represent themselves with their impressive client rosters, silently implying, "If these important names come here, we must be doing a good job." What the more recent clients may not know is that many of those people have been on the roster for years, having started with the original namesake, and their monthly fees are next to nothing as an exchange for their name value. Stars and success seem to blind the decision of clients who should be with or should stay with a small, personalized company.

For small agencies, each and every client is more than just important, they are the bread and butter—the cash flow. Small agencies cannot afford to lose a client. The amount of individual attention and quality increases proportionately with the talent and dedication of the person who owns the company.

In a large agency, the new client may be added to the mail room roster and become part of the mass mailing. Some companies will put many press releases in one envelope at a time and bill each separately; they will make a "laundry list" phone call and bill separately. The more clients an agent is representing, the more your position on her list may depend on her interest in you and/or the account.

An editor with a national daily paper told me that he will no longer take calls from the head of the entertainment department of a large, prestigious firm because all the person does is read down the entire client roster to see if there is anything that will interest the editor. If nothing strikes the editor's fancy, the publicist will insist that there must be something, and starts to read it again. Now, if the paper wants to do a story, the paper calls the agency, and begins with a strict warning to the publicist not to read down the list.

The "throw it against the wall and see what sticks" attitude is important to recognize. If you fall off the wall more than you stick, you must decide whether you want to remain because of the association with the big names (falsely believing the prestige is rubbing off on you) or leave and find yourself at the door of a small, personalized company who can give you the necessary time and nurturing that you need. Many clients begin at a small house, change to a big house when their egos grow, get lost in the shuffle, and make their way back to small houses with their tails tucked between their legs. In most cases, however, they do not return to the original house that made them. Some call it guilt, some call it pride, others just call it business.

So when do you know to move on? If the agency can no longer provide you with the services equal to your status in your field; when you no longer have the rapport you need with your agent; and when the agency can no longer obtain the necessary coverage to assist your business.

Note: Publicity alone does not make a career or sell a product. Only blame the publicists if what you give them is good and they are not reasonably able to promote what you give them.

HOW TO DECIDE WHICH COMPANY SHOULD REPRESENT YOU

The most important factor in the success of your project is the person who will be doing the hands-on work. Don't be afraid to do the following:

1. Ask who is responsible for the day-to-day elements of the campaign.
2. Ask who is going to be on the phones on your behalf.
3. Demand to meet that person. Take her out to lunch or talk with her, individually.
4. Ask her who she knows in various media and then call those names and request a performance report.
5. Call the media where you want placement and ask if they have ever heard of that account executive and if they will evaluate her performance.
6. Ask the media how they feel about the overall performance of the agency. Don't be afraid to do this.
7. Ask the media for recommendations of large and small firms and of specific account executives.
8. Insert a control clause in the contract that
   a) states your right to renegotiate your status with the firm should the approved account executive leave and
   b) enables you to cancel your contract and take your business elsewhere should the approved account executive leave.

Note: Listen carefully to the answers and pay close attention to the body language! If you are not satisfied, don't be fooled into thinking that things will change once you are their client. *Don't let your ego guide your decision just because it is a prestigious firm.*

Once you narrow your decision down to two or three choices, the criteria for choosing a PR firm become issues of personal style: how to approach, not whom to approach, how to invite, not whom to invite to your events, how to pitch, not whom to pitch.

Can You Do Your Own PR?

For Jamie Masada, owner of LA's Laugh Factory, hiring a PR agency was just throwing his money down the drain. The agency told him that only they can do what they do because they have the exclusive lists for all the media. Jamie called the Greater Los Angeles Press Club and got their membership list. He went to the newsstand, he read the papers, and he took down the writers' names. He looked in the TV guide for what network the talk shows were on and called information and got the number. He called and asked whom he should talk to about his business, and the receptionist told him. "It's as simple as that," he says. "And it doesn't cost you a penny." His advice:

SEND A PRESS RELEASE TO ALL THE MAJOR AND MINOR NEWS MEDIA, AND THEN GET ON THE PHONE YOURSELF AND CALL THEM TO FOLLOW UP. IF IT IS NEWSWORTHY FOR THEM AND THEIR AUDIENCE, THEY WILL COVER IT.

WHETHER YOU HAVE A FLOWER SHOP, A BIG COMPANY OR SMALL COMPANY, YOU MUST HAVE A WAY TO GET THE ATTENTION OF THE MEDIA, AND THAT IS VERY EASY IF YOU COME IN WITH A CREATIVE IDEA—A HOOK. IF YOU ARE NOT CREATIVE, HIRE A PERSON TO WORK WITH YOU WHO IS CREATIVE.

YOU HAVE TO BE PERSISTENT—IF YOU ARE POLITELY PERSISTENT YOU WILL SEE WONDERS!

YOU HAVE TO BE WILLING TO ASK THE MEDIA FOR HELP.

YOU HAVE TO BE ABLE TO CONVINCE THE MEDIA THAT YOU BELIEVE THAT WHAT YOU ARE SELLING IS WORTHWHILE.

ALWAYS BE HONEST.

Theoretically, you can do your own PR, because PR doesn't require miracles, a genius IQ, Spielberg creativity, or magic. Anyone, and I mean anyone, can do these basic five steps to get started: You have already accomplished step one by knowing that you want visibility, and you have accomplished step two by knowing that you want it to appear in print, on television, or on radio. Step three involves getting the address or the phone number so you can send the information, step four requires you to write or tell them what it is you want to tell them, and step five requires your putting it in the mail or dialing the phone.

The next series of tools have to do with manners, the kind you have been taught since you could point. Inquiries based on honesty and humility can usually get you past the door. Be a pest, step out of line, make demands, question decisions, whine, or try to throw your weight around, and you will get thrown out or have the door slammed in your face. Not any different than the rules the big boys need.

All media are interested in a good story, whether it be about the person who built the better mousetrap or about the better mousetrap itself. But, as with anything, there are degrees as to just how open and helpful anyone will be if they have an inkling that you don't know the first thing about playing their game. And people in the media are no different. When I asked the media, "Do you think people can do their own PR?" I got answers such as, "We are not here to baby-sit," or, "We are not here to make their job easier." There are always those who feel that because they came up through the ranks and had to deal with the populace all those years, they have paid their dues and don't have to be kind or helpful. This type would always prefer you to hire a professional so their attained position would have meaning. But there are many out there, in high places with carpeted offices, that will take your call and give you "the time of day." These are the ones who would answer the question with an emphatic yes, a vigorous nod, or vocal encouragement to participate in the personal PR process.

There was a common response after the initial reaction of yes or no. It had to do with the wish that the person seeking their attention would have a better understanding of the basic tools of courtesy and communication.

What the media doesn't like is being faced with hemming and hawing, wasted time, frivolous questions, incomplete sentences, bad writing, people who cannot take no for an answer, people who don't believe in what they are calling about, ugly persistence, demanding natures, bad listeners, people who constantly interrupt, and lack of common sense.

What they do like is the opposite of all the above.

Note: Technique is not the primary rule. The tools of communication and humanity come first. The contention is that if these are present, then the development of the technique and the tricks of the trade can't be far behind. And I can vouch for this, because when I began my career as a PR person I didn't come out of PR school, nor did I have any formal PR training. The person who offered me the job was impressed with my phone manner, my appearance, my eagerness to learn, my ability to ask pertinent questions, my ability to reason, and above all my polite manner. She figured that if I had those, it would follow that I could call and ask who was the proper person to talk to or what was the deadline or if they preferred pictures of the product instead of actual samples. So yes, you can do your own PR.

But there is one more very important step to personal PR after getting the addresses on the envelopes, licking the stamps, and sending off the inquiries. This is the part where you must follow up on your efforts to see if the media are interested in your event or story. And this is where the best laid plans oft go astray. This is where you could sabotage future success. This is where you could get in your own way. This is the part where you might not be able to do your own PR. If you can devote the necessary time and if you can stay objective, then yes, you can do your own PR. But if you find you are running out of time, if you are too busy to make the average of four phone calls for every place you have notified, if extenuating circumstances cannot allow you to commit to the responsibility of the job, if you feel that you are in way over what you can handle, or that you can't be objective...that is when you hire assistance from a competent friend or professional.

Objectivity is usually why one goes outside oneself to obtain assistance. Some of us are not affected by the closeness of a project, but others have difficulty maintaining a proper level of objectivity. It is difficult to remain calm and polite. You get persistent, rude, demanding, and before you know it you have made an enemy. This can be easily avoided by hiring a friend who can act as your publicist or representative. Gannett News "Lifestyle" reporter Barbara Nachman knows that your incredible heartfelt belief in your product usually needs to be feigned by a third party, even if it is a friend. Most media would rather talk to a third party because it is easier for them to say no to a third party. If you are representing yourself, the media might not even take your call. If they do, you may get strung along because they don't want to hurt your feelings.

According to Bob Levitan, producer of the now defunct Fritz Coleman's "It's Fritz" TV show, "If you have someone representing you, even if it's not a well-known publicist, it leaves the impression in one's mind that you've hired someone to look after your interests. Even if you use the guise of your own company, it seems more professional than if you made the call personally. It provides a perceived credibility, a less hungry approach."

What if you have the time, objectivity, and desire, but don't have the cash flow necessary to hire an agency when you realize that you need professional help? You can take an hour's consultation with a professional to assess your project. They will tell you how realistic your goals are, how the project will be perceived in the marketplace, suggest story angles, and advise you on what is the most likely media that will be open to such a project. They can help you with target mailing lists and advise you on the best way to approach the individuals in question. Then, it is up to you to do the work.

Los Angeles publicist Terri Mandell, who does just such consultations as part of her practice, knows that if you're not trained in marketing PR, your tendency is to issue a press release that says "Best yogurt shop in town." What the consultant will show you is how this approach is self-promoting and just what the media doesn't appreciate, and that the media will suggest that you buy an ad and say this yourself. Instead, the consultant might suggest that you think of sponsoring a charity drive. Start by putting a display in front of your store and handing out samples of yogurt as the foot traffic stops to read the sign. Then link up with a local celebrity to help bring more attention. When you have all this in place, then tell the media to come and do a story on the charity drive at your yogurt shop.

These are the tricks of the trade that I mentioned earlier. Maybe it will take only one meeting to show you the way, or maybe some direction by several different clients, but you'll soon get the hang of it and then, combined with some fierce envelope-licking sessions, you'll be able to do it yourself.

3

How to Make Yourself Media Friendly

"Without publicity a terrible thing happens: Nothing."
—Mike Hughs, *Publicity Express*

I don't know many people who wouldn't like to promote themselves or their businesses on television, or have a newspaper or a magazine feature them in a nicely placed story. Third-party credibility is just the thing to sell more "widgets." But just because you exist is no reason for the media to call. What you must do is cultivate yourself or your widget into being newsworthy, or what I call media friendly. Mapping out the work to get you there just takes common sense. You have something to give and there is someone who will take it, but it must be meaningful or they will discard it. You just have to figure out a way to make it meaningful. The key to most media is known as audience payoff. If it pleases the viewers or readers, they will tune in another day or buy another issue, which in turn makes the media's advertisers happy. So what you have to help them get is "more bang for their buck." One feature on you or your business appearing in the right media can get you on national television, in national magazines and newspapers, and in internationally syndicated columns. All from just one mention.

Did you know that "The Tonight Show" has a staff of researchers looking through countless newspapers and magazines to find unique guests? And that for each person found who makes it on-air, a staffer gets paid two hundred dollars?

Did you know that in order to get participants, national television talk shows put anonymous ads in the classifieds to attract people who have a story to tell?

Tabloid story "Woman Claims I.R.S. Killed Her Husband" piqued the interest of Stuart Krasnow, former booker for "The Joan Rivers Show." Three hundred thousand dollars in debt because of an IRS tax bill, the husband killed himself. Afterward, the IRS called back, said they made a billing mistake, and apologized. Krasnow also liked "Vet Says Cat Is Dead, Found Alive In Clinic Three Months Later." Such situations offer a talk show booker innumerable possibilities. Both of these people made excellent booking material as well as exciting guests on the show.

Most shows read up to ten newspapers a day looking for guests. The list includes the *New York Times,* the *Wall Street Journal, USA Today,* the *Washington Post,* the *Los Angeles Times,* the *Chicago Tribune*, and the *Atlanta Journal*, as well as local papers from all over the United States. Shows may also read thirty to fifty magazines a month, both national and local.

To get on a radio or television show, or to be interviewed by a newspaper or magazine, you usually need to have something newsworthy about you. You have to interest the media in a way that makes them consider you interesting to the potential audience. But TV and radio differ from print in that "virgins"—people who have never been on a talk show—are shied away from. Strange society, isn't it? The story "Biker women in chains by night—corporate executives by day" gets on-air, but it is difficult for the average person with no hook, no matter what his or her education or reputation. Put this thought in the back of your mind as you read on. It will make more sense as you learn more about the PR game.

So what can you do to make yourself or your business media friendly? You can:

- Devote your efforts to a charity or community organization and forge an image for yourself.
- Write a book.
- Develop a newsworthy persona outside of your primary business.
- Write editorial columns on your field of expertise for community newspapers and magazines.
- Host your own public or leased access cable show.
- Host your own radio show.
- Lecture on your field of expertise.
- Become a spokesperson for your profession or hobby.

If you can get yourself any bona fide media attention through any of the above, then you can eliminate the virgin status so feared by most media. It will show that you can deliver, that you are capable of giving a good interview, and that what you have to offer is considered an "audience payoff" by those in the know.

Creating a Positive Community Image

A video store sponsored a "Video Clip Your Child Just in Case" campaign. Parents were required to provide the blank tape and the store made a video of the child which would aid the police should the child ever be lost or abducted. A children's furniture store sponsored a similar project with finger printing children. A barber in Chicago offered to video a child's first haircut for free, and for every haircut and video he performed, he donated another haircut to a welfare or homeless child. Print, television, and radio read these releases and found the situations newsworthy. The results were national coverage for each of the three businesses. All three did their own PR, from writing the release to following up with phone calls.

To get you thinking, here are some ideas:

- If you own a beauty salon, offer lessons in hair care and beauty to those in need and/or the elderly to improve their quality of life.
- If you own a pet store, take some animals to visit a home for the elderly, an orphanage, or a hospital.
- If you run a green nursery, offer saplings to children and get the city to let them plant the saplings on public property.
- If you own a video store, set up a free or low-cost lending library for an orphanage or the elderly.
- If you own a boat, organize boat trips for inner city children.
- If you are a carpenter, unite with a home improvement store and your local government and build pocket parks for neighborhood children. Involve the parents, older siblings, and local volunteers.
- If you play an instrument, give free lessons to the disabled.

Then, let the media know. There is nothing out of line in your wanting to be able to reach out into the community and have people notice. If the intent is pure, good always comes back to you. Your deeds are always recognized by the media as usable. They know that you are trying to get visibility, of course, but it seems to soften the blow when that effort has some good deed attached to it. If you give something back to the community where you make money, the media will be more inclined to look twice when you want some coverage.

Marsha McDonald owns an ad agency in Memphis, Tennessee. For their fifth anniversary she put up five thousand dollars for prize money and asked the Memphis School System's fifth graders to create posters about an element of their city that they liked. A local printer printed the posters, a local bank exhibited them, and the media judged them. The agency, the bank, and the printer all got coverage in one way or another, proving that community involvement can lead to great PR.

Note: Nonprofit organizations can use Public Service Announcements as a way to get media visibility. PSAs are the TV and radio commercials about drunk driving, AIDS, etc. There is a local and network regulated format that must be adhered to. You can find out the format information by calling your local station and asking for their public affairs office. They can give you advice about requirements and how to proceed.

Having Your Book Published

In many circles, being published is the next best thing to having a statue erected in your honor in the town square. Being published can afford you instant career and personal recognition, credibility, authority in your field, client appreciation, monetary compensation, and job promotion at your workplace. It can open many doors that you could not have dreamed of entering before. One of these doors is to the media. When you are published, you automatically become a spokesperson for your field of expertise. Whether it is for a disaster or a general information call, those who are published are usually consulted for a comment by the media. This exposure has great potential for advancing one's business or career. Being published also affords you the opportunity to go out on the lecture circuit or to appear on community or issue oriented television. If you have something to say, whether it be for the public, your field, or just your clientele, don't underestimate the power of being published. If you don't think you can write the material, there are many independent writers for hire.

There are several books that can guide you through the publishing maze. I found *The Insider's Guide to Book Editors and Publishers 1990-1991* by Jeff Herman to be the most helpful. In addition to listing publishers and editors and what they are looking for, it explains how to get an agent and how to write a proposal, and includes a supplementary reading list. Another useful guide to getting published is the *Writer's Market*. Both books should be available at most libraries and bookstores.

There are two major reference guides available in your public library: 1. *Literary Market Place (LMP)*, 121 Chanlon Road, New Providence, New Jersey, 07974, (908) 665-2840, and 2. *Publishers Weekly*, 245 E. 17th Street, New York, New York, 10011, (212) 645-9700. *LMP* contains names and addresses of publishers with a breakdown of the categories they publish (e.g., poetry, how-to, cookbooks, fiction, etc.) as well as agents and other publishing services. *Publishers Weekly* reports on the current books, trends, courses, events, and industry news. Both sources present less difficult and time-consuming research options than camping out at your local bookstore and copying down names and addresses.

Should the publishing houses not make a move to publish your book, you could consider the self-publishing route. But be forewarned that self-publishing (also known as "vanity publishing") can be a much riskier process because you assume much of what would otherwise be a publisher's burden, financially and otherwise. The other side to this coin is that you are in control of your product from beginning to end, including content and financial statements. If you are the kind of person who demands this type of arena, then by all means self-publish.

And don't indulge in feelings of insecurity or of being second best, or viewing self-publishing as only a last resort because the core industry has turned you down: More and more people are self-publishing because they can take control of their product's destiny as well as the purse strings. Keep in mind that your goal is to have a concrete means to approach the media, and, as such, either way of publishing allows you to do just that.

Many publishing sources will direct you to companies that will help you self-publish. One such company is Para Publishing, whose founder, Dan Poynter, guides the neophyte through the entire process with the aid of seminars, books, and computer software. *Contact:* Para Publishing, Mr. Dan Poynter, P.O. Box 4232, Santa Barbara, California 93103. (805) 968-7277.

American Book Trade Directory and *Publishers & Distributors* will help you line up distributors, wholesalers, and bookstores. *Contact:* Bowker Publishing: 121 Chanlon Road, New Providence, New Jersey, 07974. (908) 665-2840.

Developing a Newsworthy Persona Outside of Your Primary Business

What you do for a living may not be newsworthy or interesting to the media. If that's the case, you must develop a secondary approach. Sometimes it comes from a hobby and sometimes it is just a creative idea that springs forth as an offshoot from what you do for a living. Go over your likes and dislikes, your dreams and your aspirations, because lurking under that everyday nine-to-five world can be the road that will take you to media heaven.

These three people took their basic talents and created another side of themselves, bringing them media coverage that led them to monetary success, visibility, and more opportunities:

Publicist Terri Mandell developed a lecture series, entitled "Power Schmoozing," on how to promote yourself at gatherings and meetings. As a result of her being written up in the

"Peoplescape" section of *Los Angeles Magazine* she was offered a book deal and invited to appear on television.

When video producer, lecturer, and author Michael Wiese moved to Los Angeles, he knew that being noticed immediately was no easy feat in a town packed with people who do what he does, so he developed and published a board game similar to Monopoly called "Goin' Hollywood." It was all about getting your movie produced, any way you can. With *Premiere* magazine purchasing five hundred games for movie studio Christmas presents and *Video* magazine giving it to the video production companies, the entire movie and video industry owned that game by Christmas. Coupled by the massive international multimedia coverage gotten when the game was released, he had immediate recognition in his new hometown.

While waiting for clients to knock down the door of her newly formed PR agency, B. L. Ochman used her knowledge as a Fortune 500 publicist to create "Rent-a-Kvetch," an artful, legitimate way of getting the complaints of the everyday person directly to those who head America's corporations. The name and premise immediately caught the fancy of the media, leading to appearances on talk and magazine shows, interviews with the *New York Times* and *People* magazine, and a book deal, as well. This exposure got her a client base. A newly acquired client said he hired her because, "Anyone who can generate that much publicity for themselves must be great."

Writing Editorials and Columns

A two-thousand-word column can cost you anywhere from one to five thousand dollars, depending on the magazine or newspaper's rates. Many local and regional outlets offer free space for local professionals to contribute a column, an editorial, or commentary on a pertinent or timely subject.

Why? In many cases it enables the media to have stories or "copy" without maintaining a staff. With professionals and highly visible people writing for them, it appears that the outlet is a good place to be seen, thereby enhancing its image.

Writing a commentary, an editorial, or a column is not difficult. Traditionally these encompass trends, problems, or innovations in content. The exposure is invaluable in promoting your business as well as yourself, and affords you the visibility for other media to see you and find out what you do.

But before you go off and write, you should call the individual media you want to appear in and query them on your idea. It can eliminate a lot of wasted time, effort, and emotions on both ends. If you need to have your materials returned, mark that you want them returned, and enclose a self-addressed, stamped envelope. This will improve your chances of getting the materials back.

When your commentary, editorial, or column is published, make a copy of it. This is the beginning of your media kit. The reprinted copy will show other media that you have already established credibility in the media marketplace and that you have something to say.

Creating Your Own TV or Radio Show

PUBLIC AND LEASED ACCESS

Creating your own television or radio show automatically makes for acceptable self-promotion. Many on-air personalities who have appeared on such shows as "The Tonight Show," "The Joan Rivers Show," and "Late Night with David Letterman" first appeared on public access cable and radio shows. Psychologist Barbara De Angelis, author of *Making Love Work*, began her media career by buying air time on KFOX radio. She parlayed her spokesperson status from someone in the community to one on the "Home Show," then to her own one-hour, daily, national network television show.

After representing a singing telegram company for two years, I had exhausted all feature and repeat story avenues. But when I suggested they produce a cable show televising singing telegrams to the recipient, not only was it an instant success, but their antics became a staple in the gossip, lifestyle, and commentary columns, prompting reoccurring visits on local talk shows.

There are two cable divisions—leased and public access, the difference between them being the intent. Public access time is basically free, but there is a small handling fee to anyone who wants to produce a *noncommercial* show to air on the local cable system. This means you cannot mention prices or specific retail outlets. Leased access, the *commercial* outlet of the same local cable system, charges a nominal fee for the time, during which you can use it to promote anything you please, including selling the time to advertisers or other clients.

The shows on either channel provide a wealth of possibilities to promote yourself. On cable channels, you'll find people reading plays, discussing political platforms and issues, and investigating health and nutrition. They give astrology readings, voice therapy, cooking lessons, and teach chiropractic techniques. Cable television is truly a worthwhile investment in time, effort, and money to promote yourself. And, it's easy! Basically, for both leased and public access, all you have to do is go in, pick out an available time slot, and satisfy the channel's individual monetary requirements. Most stations give an orientation and a workshop on how to produce your own show, as well as providing a studio with hands-on equipment training and script development classes. Although the show is pretty much yours, it does have to abide by the local company's rules for standards and decency. Cable systems are not standardized so call for procedures and pricing. You can find the cable systems and stations listed in the telephone directory.

BUYING TALK SHOW RADIO TIME

Radio is another way to promote yourself. You can buy time with the only criterion being how the topic incorporates itself within the guidelines of the station's programming day. To determine which stations do what types of programming, go to your library and find *Standard Rate and Data*—there is one for radio and one for television. Another source is the *Directory of Broadcast Media*. These directories give all the information anyone could possibly want or need about the makeup of every station. For talk shows, you'll want to target AM stations—they are the ones that do the most of this type of programming. Not all talk stations will list this on-air time capability, so call and ask if you don't see it specifically listed.

Note: When you call the station, remember that on-air time is different from the buying and selling of "time." The latter indicates that you want to advertise. *Contact:* Standard Rate and Data: 3004 Glenview Road, Wilmette, Illinois 60091. (708) 256-6067. *Contact:* Directory of Broadcast Media: Gale Research, 835 Penobscot Building, Detroit, Michigan 48226. (313) 961-2242.

Once they accept your programming concept, you must pay a small fee for studio rental. Most stations will provide technical assistance for the show's production, if required.

Note: Make certain that you own the program. It is always wise to have a lawyer look at the contracts. If you do own the program, you are free to solicit other stations in other cities and states. This is a form of "syndication." In essence, you can create your own radio network by "bicycling" them yourself (mailing them out to each station, getting them back after broadcast, and sending them on to the next station), using a satellite uplink facility, or hiring a company that specializes in such transmissions. Publicity Express in San Francisco is such a company. *Contact:* Publicity Express, 1563 Solano Avenue No. 223, Berkeley, California 94707. (800) 541-2897.

Being able to show that you know how to interview and conduct yourself in a professional manner puts you far ahead of the pack when you are looking to garner media attention.

Lecturing

Establishing yourself as a lecturer is another stepping stone in acquiring publicity for yourself. Dotty Walters is the common person's guru in this field with her book *Speak and Grow Rich*, seminars on how to be a lecturer, and her monthly magazine *Sharing Ideas*. It all started when, as a real estate agent, she was asked by local community organizations to discuss special topics of the real estate industry. Soon she began to get requests from all over the area to speak, which led to community television and radio appearances, thus increasing her business and personal recognition tenfold. Now she travels around the world, giving seminars and promoting others through her speaker service. There are many speaker bureaus throughout the country—look in your phone book or call your local professional organizations, which may have relationships with the bureaus.

Note: Did you know that there are speaker bureaus that will book you into cruise ship lectures? And you thought you had found heaven on the Lions Club–Chamber of Commerce–Rotarian speakers circuit!

If your material is controversial or innovative, the media may be interested in what you have to say. Let them know you are speaking—they may not come and report live, but if you pique their interest perhaps they will invite you on a segment of their own, or call you the next time your field of expertise is needed.

Establishing Yourself as a Spokesperson

Actor Gene Wilder now alerts the public to little-known early warning tests that may save women from dying of ovarian cancer, a condition from which his wife, Gilda Radner, might not have died had she been aware of it sooner. A woman with a family history similar to Radner's saw Connie Chung interview Wilder on TV and because of the tests he advocated, she was able to get early treatment for a life-threatening disease.

The information you have to offer may contribute to saving lives, educate, enrich, or encourage a change in people's perspective, and the media in these cases is always open. The message here is to seize the opportunity. This is no time for being shy. This is a wonderful way for you to get media visibility for yourself as well as for your profession, organization, or ideas.

For instance, your local news reports on someone who has a nervous breakdown in the middle of the downtown shopping center, or on a husband who beats his wife because he is overloaded with stress. You are a psychologist who specializes in stress-related problems. Call the media and offer your expertise.

The news is filled with stories about toxins in landfills, chemical water pollution, and waste seepage. You install and service septic tanks or build and install wells and storm drains. Call the media and offer your expertise.

The news is filled with stories about gardening with pesticides, rehabilitating the soil, and food restrictions from toxicity. You own an organic farm. Call the media and offer your expertise.

The news is filled with a celebrity divorce and you are a local matrimonial lawyer who specializes in prenuptial agreements. You know what to do.

Almost every media person I spoke with said yes to the possibility of accepting a call from someone with credentials on a subject pertinent to the news of the day. You don't have to be published to discuss ground toxins seeping into septic tanks or water wells—you can be the repairman who sees the results on a twenty-four-hour basis. If you can offer direct, factual and authoritative commentary for the subject at hand, call your local television station, the radio station, or the paper.

This is your moment. One call could catapult you into that role of consultant to the media. You could be quoted, interviewed, and used as a role model. It could also give you the tools you need to parlay your role out of the local scene and into the national one.

When you call, remember to be in the moment. As Marianne Goldstein, assistant city desk editor of the *New York Post,* said, "What's the worst that can happen? They'll say no." The procedure is not difficult. All media phone numbers are listed in the telephone directory or can be gotten through information. Usually an intern or a desk assistant will take your call, and although they don't make the decisions, they'll take your name, number, and reason for calling, and get back to you after they give the information to the news director.

You've seen that little outlined box that accompanies the central story in newspapers and magazines? It is called a sidebar. Sometimes it is an anecdote, or list of things to do or to know. If you hit the editor at the right time with the right stuff, you or the information you have to impart can be that sidebar. Even if you think it's a stretch, try it. It never hurts to try. It may be just the punch that the editor or programmer is looking for. All you need is one thing to begin that media kit. And it's highly unlikely that they will come to you if they don't know you exist.

Lyle Gregory of "The Michael Jackson Show" offers these pointers, appropriate to all media, when you call as a spokesperson in an emergency–phone pitch situation. Write down what you want to say so you will get it out accurately without forgetting a detail that may make or break your pitch.

You probably have only ten to fifteen seconds to state your case or why you are calling. Don't hem and haw—they will hang up on you. Know ahead of time what you want to tell them that you know, and most of all why it will be of interest to their audience. They don't have time to pump you for the hook or the reason you're calling, and if they have to pull it out of you they most probably will not take you seriously. Immediately identify yourself and your purpose. Get into what you have to say very quickly, don't chitchat, and don't be cute—this is no time for humor. Don't call to get on the show unless you have a direct relationship with that topic.

If you've gone this far, *don't forget to leave your name and number*! If they're embroiled, ask if a day or two later is better timing. You don't know what's going on in the boiler room, nor do they have time to tell you about it. If they are in the middle of a news crisis they may forget you called, so call back. Besides, they may have misplaced your number and would like to talk to you when things calm down.

Note: The news business frequently trades in here-today-gone-tomorrow issues. News happens every day, and if you wait two days or a week, the show may be on to something else. So make that call. If you don't know when to call, call immediately. They'll tell you when to call back or they'll take your name and number and get back to you.

In order to maximize your efforts and stay in their consciousness, send them a letter telling them who you are, and if you have a brochure or other media support materials send them along, too. Show them how you can be a source, either on camera or off camera. Contribute to their bank of knowledge. If the issue is germinating but soon will be a full-blown concern to the public, send along articles that cross-reference the issue you are pitching so that they can see that it is in fact important and newsworthy. What this does, aside from alerting them to the existence of a deeper topic, is give them lead time to watch the issue grow to where it might become a breaking news item for them. This can make you a valuable news source and credible authority for their programming needs.

Another route used to establish yourself as an expert or spokesperson is to list yourself in the resource guide used by over six thousand radio, TV, and print media. Broadcast Interview Source publishes the *Directory of Experts, Authorities and Spokespersons*, an "encyclopedia of sources" containing listings of over fourteen hundred associations, corporations, trade groups, and individuals from all fifty states who are available for media contact, involving any topic from AIDS to grief, from gums to zoos. This reference book is made available to every TV, print, and radio outlet. *Contact:* Directory of Experts, Authorities and Spokespersons, Broadcast Interview Source, 2233 Wisconsin Avenue N.W. No. 406, Washington, D.C. 20007-4104. (202) 333-4904.

You can register yourself as an expert witness with the National Forensic Services Directory and their computer bank, which is accessed primarily by lawyers looking for professionals to testify in court cases. *Contact:* National Forensic Services Directory, 17 Temple Terrace, Lawrenceville, N.J. 08648. (609) 883-0550.

And, should you be a part of a unique organization dealing with a special topic, list yourself in the *Encyclopedia of Associations* or the *Consultants and Consulting Organizations Directory.* Gale Research publishes over 215 directories, many of which are in this genre. *Contact:* Gale Research, 835 Penobscot Building, Detroit, Michigan 48226. (313) 961-2242.

4

How to Get the Media to Cover Your Event

"If you can provide me with a 'REALLY, I DIDN'T KNOW THAT' response I'll be sure to cover it. All others must stand in line."
—Bob Levitan, producer, "It's Fritz"

Once upon a time we would only have to whisper about an event and the media would show up in droves. But with the number of outlets shrinking through mergers and bankruptcy, the media playground is definitely not what it used to be. Whereas once a town had both a morning and evening daily paper, more and more we have become a one-paper town. Staffs are reduced and papers are subscribing to syndications and media services for prefab stories. True, there are more TV and radio shows, but even they are interested in the big names—the stars. "Little guys" have a difficult time getting a shot on a local morning show, and not all regions have community, business, or home shows. The good news is that there are more regional papers and suburban papers that do interviews with the little guy on the way up, and there are radio stations but the shows are for targeted markets. All of these small-scale and targeted outlets are good places to be, but what you may really want is coverage where the big people play—in the daily papers and on the local TV and radio news shows. Getting into the broad-reach media has become more difficult because of the media's need to hold their audience with sensationalism and popular figures.

And so we are faced with the dilemma of how to get the attention of the media for the masses. Now we assume the position next to Rodin's *The Thinker* as we delve deep into our inner core to find the right spark of creativity to tempt the person responsible for assignments.

Let me share with you some sparks of creativity that have been used to tempt the media. It's *Gypsy*'s Miss Mezzeppa who was right on the button when she sang the song "You Gotta Have a Gimmick." We call it a hook—something interesting that will "hook" the media. When you read these examples, try to see beyond the particular example and imagine how the hook can be adapted to your own project. Creativity and its potential application are what I want you to be aware of, not the category of client for which it was created.

Hooks

There is a legend about a PR agent who, over fifty years ago, marched a real elephant, dressed in a pink tutu, into the press room of the *Los Angeles Daily News*, heralding the fact that their company had a nose for news. There is another elephant story that makes news every year when the Ringling Brothers, Barnum & Bailey Circus comes to New York City. Prompted by a suggestion from their PR agent, the circus walks an elephant, amidst clowns and fanfare, from New Jersey, where their train stops, through the Lincoln Tunnel to the New York side, and then on to Madison Square Garden, flanked by adoring fans.

To jazz up a campaign for the Marilyn Monroe Doll, I suggested that the higher priced porcelain version of the doll be outfitted with a fur coat designed by a famous furrier, diamond earrings and pendant by a famous jeweler, and hair and makeup by a well-known cosmetician; that the porcelain version be a limited edition, with the mold destroyed after production of the final number; and that the price for this version be set at $5,000. These improvements would not only get the client the trade press he desired, but it had the potential of putting him in every media outlet from here to Tasmania and back, not to mention the toy industry history books.

When it came time for the unveiling, the media conference photo opportunity was like a zoo on a Sunday. We were heavily attended by the international trade and consumer press. But it was nothing compared to what occurred when the doll was delivered to New York's most fashionable toy store, F.A.O. Schwarz. We hired a Brinks armored truck with two uniformed, armed men. Arriving at the toy store, they cautiously stepped from the truck and scanned the crowd for possible lurking thieves who might snatch the doll before it made it into the store. Of course they were greeted not by thieves but by a cadre of media who snapped, rolled, talked into microphones, and took notes. It made all six of the early and late evening news programs, the cover of the *New York Daily News*, stories in *Time*, as well as picture stories in magazines all over the world. It was picked up and carried by every domestic and international wire service. The limited porcelain edition sold out in one week to collectors and buyers like the man from Saudi Arabia who saw the story in the International Edition of the *Herald Tribune* and faxed in an order for six dolls.

Los Angeles publicist Dick Delson worked on *The Unholy*, a horror movie about demonic possession. To promote the film he arranged to have a woman hypnotized, placed in a glass coffin, and buried alive outside the movie theater. The movie was not going to get coverage in and of itself—nobody in the media cared! But it was the stunt, the hook, that brought out the media in droves. The amount of coverage Delson was able to generate was truly unbelievable for the size of the event.

The Laugh Factory's Jamie Masada donated Mylar blankets to the homeless when the Los Angeles temperature dropped to an unusual thirty degrees. He sent out releases to all media, but targeted Top Forty radio stations with an announcement that he would donate a blanket with each admission to the comedy club. He included several punch lines, exclusive to each station, instructing them to use them as their own when they announced the blanket giveaway. He got one hundred percent pickup and a crowded club.

Los Angeles' Julian Meyers was one of many publicists assigned to the 1950 gala premiere of Twentieth Century-Fox's *All About Eve* at the then Grauman's Chinese Theater (now called Mann's Chinese Theater). In order to attract the media attention that would make this premiere stand out from all the rest, he arranged for the nearby Hotel Roosevelt to darken all the letters in their sign except the E, V, and E. This appeared in the major gossip columns, making a perfect "column item."

To create unusual visibility for a client at a trade show in New York City, Los Angeles publicist Don Garrett hired eight horse-drawn hansom cabs for the run of the conference. He had each cab equipped with a six-foot-tall replica of an old-fashioned electrified streetlight with the company logo suspended on a shingle under the lamp. Whenever his delegates needed to go anywhere, the logoed hansom cab would be there to take them. Trade photographs and bonus photo coverage from the New York City papers gave him a marketing tool for his next mailing piece.

For New York City Country Music Day, the type of event in which it is very difficult to get more than just advanced listings, I convinced the client to spring for promotional dollars to put on a midtown lunch-hour parade two weeks in advance of the date. I hired four stagecoaches, eight horses and riders, a flatbed truck with a country music band, and a huge banner promoting the upcoming event. One hundred percent pickup on all local news shows, and double-spread centerfolds in both local papers the next day.

B. L. Ochman did a number of promotions for supermarket magnate Stew Leonard's Betsy's Bakery. For her ingenious

"Cookie Pen Pals," she had schoolchildren write letters to sailors from the local area and put the letters in boxes of cookies from Betsy's Bakery. She invited the media to the letter-writing box-stuffing day at school where the cookie cargo was loaded into the Stew Leonard Cow Truck that moos when you beep the horn. It got excellent local coverage, and it had just the right angle to attract a national feed.

For the twenty-fifth anniversary celebration of the Mark Tapper Forum Theater in Los Angeles, publicist Nan Miller wrapped the entire building in aluminum foil, surrounded it with a huge bow, and placed twenty-five oversize electric candles on the roof. Media coverage included an article on the theater's twenty-five years and a picture of "the cake."

Invitations

Yes, even party and event invitations themselves are considered hooks. Glitter is a major way to get attention. Everyone has at one time opened a release or invitation that contained some form of glitter. And as they watched it sink into their carpet or become embedded in the fabric of their clothing, they vowed that if they ever get their hands on the person who sent it... Even the thoughtful warning "Glitter Inside" will automatically earn your release-invitation a toss. But the effect of glitter is so appropriately festive, I created little sealed packets of glitter and stuffed them inside the invitations so that I could keep the idea of glitter without annoying the media. It got me many thank-you calls. Good hook, huh?

Publicist Don Garrett got the media to open an invitation once by printing "No Noodles Inside" on the envelope.

Then there was the red, dynamite stick–shaped tube, complete with a burned wick, stuffed with a scorched piece of parchment and printed with the party particulars written in Old English script.

How about the expensive bottle of champagne with the invitation printed as the label?

Or the Christmas party invitation which is really a letter from Santa hand addressed to the media person?

Then there was the arts supply company that was opening its first New York City store. Publicist B. L. Ochman called all the graphic designers and asked them what they did to have fun at a party (also asking if she could quote them). When the invitation came, rolled up inside a three-foot-long, hot pink tube, it was a three-foot-by-three-foot hot pink piece of paper, covered with quotes on "how graphic designers have fun." "Bill G. looks forward to eating all the cashews out of the nut mix." "Sam H. likes to steal the silverware." "Mary C. loves to dance to Motown music." The invitation was sent to two thousand people in the graphic design and related industry, and almost everyone said they would attend. After all, if all those graphic designers had put their names on the invitation, then it must be a happening event. The client received over one million dollars of commercial business after that party and got wonderful trade coverage. Just what the client ordered.

But a word to the wise from the *New York Daily News*'s Liz Rittersporn, who takes umbrage at invitations that come in a big box taped like there is no tomorrow. "I slave away with the knife and scissors and get the tape stuck to my fingers and clothes, I almost break a nail, and then I have to deal with those foam peanuts that cling to my black sweater. All for what? Inevitably there is a little cheap wicker or porcelain basket that I don't want, with an invitation to a party that I don't want to attend. This is enough to gain admittance to my 'you know what list,' or nothing short of banishment if I broke a nail…" Do not take this barrage lightly—it is an opinion shared by many.

Parties

Another hook is to throw a party. Take the charity party that was thrown in a New York City subway tunnel, or the extravaganza held on board the aircraft carrier *Intrepid*, docked on New York's Hudson River, for example. If you are going to use a party for a hook, the only advice I can give you is it better be big or very interesting. Parties, in my estimation, are not the way to go. I have found that parties are usually (but not always) for the publicist's or the client's ego.

Note: Many media people told me that the only parties they like to go to are those where there will be people they *want* to meet. Many media people will give the invitation to their staff and tell them to collect any promotional materials. Very rarely will the media cover a party unless it is filled with stars or local civic or business officials who are usually difficult to contact, or if something newsworthy is supposed to happen.

But if the party is to launch a product? You can usually count on the trade press coming, but usually not the consumer press.

Now, if you combine the party with a charitable cause, you have a better chance of getting consumer press, but many times they will eliminate the sponsor's name and just report on the cause. Be careful—ask yourself if it isn't only your ego that wants the party. It is interesting to note the increase in charity parties once it became known that it was a good way to get media attention. Now most newspapers have a column dedicated to charity events. I guess it worked!

News Conferences

News conferences are preferred over parties as a means to get the media to pay attention. Those who give them feel that news conferences are more credible in the eyes of the media. However, it is the consensus of the media and the PR industry that news conferences are a waste of time, effort, and talent unless you are ready to announce something genuinely important, and most everyone I've interviewed agreed that very few of us have news of the magnitude that would warrant bringing out the media's troops. The rule of thumb seems to be that if you can get your message across in a news release, use a news *release*, not a news conference.

Don't have a news conference or media gathering if all you are going to do is give a prepared speech and leave, allowing no time for questions and answers. You could have saved the media, and yourself, a great deal of frustration by sending out a print or video release. Some even consider such conferences a slap in the face and the ultimate in self-serving behavior. Needless to say, this can damage your image.

Jane Gilman, editor of the *Larchmont Chronicle*, feels that news conferences, for the most part, are manufactured news, and she doesn't like to be duped by them.

In the opinion of Mary Lyons of Associated Press Audio, news conferences provide nice opportunities to visit with other reporters who they don't get a chance to see around town. Other than that they are usually boring and self-serving until the good questions begin.

Editor Brian Lewis feels that news conferences foster "herd" journalism. He hates them. "It's worse than a press release because it's the only way you're going to get it and it's all managed and packaged. It's like a dog and pony show."

Patty Neger, a booker for "Good Morning America," refuses to go unless it is a potential competitive booking situation and the person she wants to get for the show is there, or if she can't get to their PR person by phone and will be able to confront him or her there. What else would make her go? "I would only go if it is a Miss America stepping down, a sports figure who is resigning or being indicted, or for hostages who have just been released."

There are two types of news conferences, general calls and one-on-ones. The general call is a formal presentation of information after which the speaker may or may not answer questions from the media. The one-on-one takes place after the initial information presentation and is choreographed as a private moment in which individuals from the media can question the speaker face to face, eliminating the possibility of not being called on during a question and answer period. The one-on-one is the preferred method for many reasons, especially because of the potential for getting exclusive information. Technically, the reporter doesn't have to worry that there are not enough plug-in facilities for his microphone and camera, and he doesn't have to share footage and run the risk of the other stations' logo and voice appearing in his segment. Visually and by ear it allows the reporter to craft the moment for his audience, as well as make it look and feel original, exclusively for them. The chances are greater that the interview can be held for publication or broadcast at a later date, should the news conference segment be preempted. The one-on-one interview can be saved for file footage, and if you continue to be newsworthy it can be used in future stories.

Note: With a one-on-one interview, remember to establish the time frame before the interview begins. That way everyone knows the time parameters and there are no surprises when you call for a closing statement five minutes before the time is up.

Every media person interviewed agreed that if they were offered a one-on-one with the opportunity to only ask one or two questions, they would prefer an organized news conference where everyone is present. This would automatically increase the number of questions, giving them the opportunity for a broader picture. So if you do decide to hold a one-on-one, do it to allow for a real interview opportunity, not just to placate the media.

DEADLINES: NEWS CONFERENCE DILEMMAS TO WATCH OUT FOR!

Unless absolutely necessary, try not to have a news conference after noon on a Friday. If a paper doesn't have a weekend edition, the news is old and unusable by Monday. If you call the papers on Thursday with an advance you could score points, but if you do that, the news will appear in the papers the morning of the news conference, betraying the news for those who will show up. That undermines your intent.

Don't hold news conferences during the media's closing or deadline times. Find out what is the last possible time to make the early evening TV news, the late editions of newspapers, and so on. Decide what media are most important and what timing is best for you, then schedule accordingly.

"Think of what will go in the next day's paper. Give me someone who is quotable, give me something to hang a story on. Don't just give a press conference and expect me to come up with what the story is," says Marianne Goldstein of the *New York Post*. As she reminded me, "That's what reporters do, they look for news and they report it. Don't just hand me a dead fish and tell me to make sushi!"

"Reporters are not out to make you look or sound bad. Usually. We are out to get your message compatible with our medium. We are there to facilitate your message to our audience as long as your message is interesting, memorable, quotable, audience attracting, irresistible, image laden, all of those things, presumably considered in advance," says Jack Popejoy of KFWB radio in Los Angeles.

Jack Popejoy also wants you to know that the question and answer period that follows your formal presentation is your best sales opportunity. A good salesperson will tell you that you don't begin actually making the sale until the customer begins asking the questions. Your first customer in the media is the reporter. Your ultimate sale is the audience of his or her publication or broadcast, but you have to sell the media on your message first.

If you think that your part of the news conference is over when you've completed your presentation and have begun inviting questions, you will be very disappointed in the media coverage that you get afterward. Because you are going to be speaking much more naturally when you are responding to questions, radio and television are more inclined to use those responses rather than your prepared statement. Don't think that your part and your work is over when you have finished your presentation. The part that is most likely to survive, to be quoted, to be broadcast, will be your responses to the media's questions.

PITFALLS OF A GENERAL CALL NEWS CONFERENCE

In line with Ms. Neger's reason for going, I have never been a fan of giving general call news conferences because of the variables that could undermine the necessary success. There are weather, last-minute scheduling conflicts, media family problems or illnesses, poor site choice, travel restrictions, crew vehicle breakdowns, boredom and, of course, natural disasters. When asked if they have given many news conferences that didn't work, most publicists reply, "The question is: Did we ever have a lot that worked?" Here are some of the classic examples of why not to call a news conference.

Supermarket magnate Stew Leonard's daughter runs his quarter-million-dollar-a-week bakery department. Mr. Leonard's opinion was that his daughter's personal cookie recipe, for Betsy's Bakery cookies, was the best in the world. So publicist B. L. Ochman invited customers and the regional media to a taste test using Mrs. Field's cookies, David's cookies, and Betsy's Bakery cookies. The event turned into a publicist's nightmare: her client lost. The moral: Do a dry run without the media. If it doesn't turn out to your advantage, you can always cancel the conference (or you can not schedule it in the first place).

Then there is the classic story about a cat food company that rented the ballroom of New York City's prestigious Waldorf-Astoria to announce a new brand of cat food. The gist of the event was that, on cue, fifty cats were to be led on stage where they would take their places at banquet tables set with fine china, crystal, and ice sculptures of cats. But the humans didn't remember that even for trained cats, noise, cameras, and bright lights are not favorite things, and so when the cue to take their places was given, rather than go to the tables, they went under the tables or ran away. The event was staged to show the media how delicious the cats found the product, but when the cats wouldn't cooperate, a mortified president of the company proceeded to convince the media anyway by eating the cat food himself.

Actor Herve Villechaize instructed publicist Flo Selfman to devise a way he could raise relief money for victims of the 1979 Algerian earthquake. Thinking to take advantage of the actor's height—three feet, ten inches—in comparison to the task he was undertaking, she planned to use the gigantic size of the Goodyear blimp as backdrop to a press conference. The press conference was held at the blimp base, a good hour from Los Angeles. No press representatives or photographers came. Moral: Think about how far the media must travel to do the story. Plan the conference at a convenient location or supply transportation.

A publicist friend of mine represented a consultant who assisted corporations in buying art for their offices. To increase her client's visibility she suggested an annual mone-tary arts award for young artists plus placement of their pieces in the lobby of a corporation. Another PR agent's nightmare. No media showed up—in fact, no one showed up, not even her mother. She recalls the day as being horrible. It seems that someone else in the art field held an event at the same time with more star names. Moral: Don't overestimate your client's worth, and don't inflate your own ego by thinking you can attract the media. Send releases on the information and when the art is hung, have a cocktail party in the lobby. You can often count on media to show up where there is food.

NEWS CONFERENCE EDIBLES, THE OFT-FORGOTTEN ISSUE

If you insist on having a news conference, you must pay attention to the food. And I say this with great seriousness.

Marianne Goldstein, *New York Post* assistant city desk

editor, reminded me of the joke that says, "If it isn't catered, it isn't journalism."

Rhonda Markowitz of MTV's News Department has as her credo: "You want to feed and water the media people whenever possible."

If the news conference is in the morning, provide a good cup of coffee and a sweet roll. For lunch, perhaps a deli spread. Don't serve anything that's messy. Also, it is usually a good idea to plan a menu that will accommodate vegetarians.

You are probably wondering why I have spent time on the subject of food. Well, food is a big joke at news conferences. The media's dealing with the seriousness of the news event is often secondary to the issue of rating the food. So that the food does not interfere or detract, make sure it is simple, adequate, and unobtrusive. Guarantee that your news conference comes first.

Events

Another hook to attract the media is to stage an event. All events are hooks to get publicity for a cause, an organization, a political philosophy, a person, place, or thing. By an event, I mean a charity auction, a gambling party, or a ninth race at your local racetrack including your friend's horses with those of the track. An event is a wonderfully legitimate way to exploit the virtues of almost anything. Events, however, do not always get the media "off their duff." What kinds of events pique the interest of the media enough for them to want to attend in person and write an interesting article soon after? The consensus among the media was:

- If you invite them to a thousand-dollar-a-plate dinner where they are going to meet rich and famous people to whom they don't usually have access (the media doesn't pay for the dinner).

- If the event is truly special, and stands above the commonplace.
- If it is a social, nonbusiness environment where people can have fun and not expect to be pitched to death.
- If they know that, besides their friends, the movers and shakers in the community will be there and they can get to mingle with them, pick up story ideas, talk to people, keep in touch with what is going on in the community.
- If they can learn something.

If you plan on the event selling itself, you are under a serious misconception, unless the particular media you are contacting has a column or prearranged assignment. Most, if not all, event publicity is done so that information on the event appears immediately before the event to get people to attend, as opposed to after the event when, although it is nice, it doesn't sell tickets this year. This will be discussed in greater depth in the chapter on pitching.

Celebrities can be a big media draw. Did you know that even if you live in Scranton, Pennsylvania, that you could get a Hollywood star to come to your fund-raising dinner? Barry Greenberg, president of Celebrity Connection, works with all types of agencies in obtaining celebrity participation for anywhere in the world. If you want them to speak at a function, be a spokesperson for a cause, or enjoy themselves at the prerace party at the Kentucky Derby, he can arrange it, for a fee, of course.

The modern-day marriage of celebrities to events was ordained when Greenberg saw the amount of media coverage he was able to get for a charity he was consulting when he asked a famous neighbor to attend. Now he helps raise millions of dollars for charities and all types of organizations through matching celebrities with events.

What's in it for the celebrity besides money and a trip to nowhere? Don't feel guilty if you bring a celebrity to your small town, because celebrities know that using these events is a good way to create a winning situation for both the celebrity and the event. It enables them to get more mileage for themselves and their career and it shines a light on an organization that might not otherwise be there. When the booker on the "Tonight Show" asks what they can talk about and they say they can talk about their television character, that's one thing. But when they say they can also talk about the fact they are the spokesperson for a charity, that gives an entirely new dimension to the celebrity. The charity gets the notoriety and the celebrity enhances his or her visibility quotient and career.

5

How to Plan Your Media Campaign

"You gotta have a gimmick!"
—Miss Mezzeppa, *Gypsy*

You go after media visibility for one or two basic reasons, to increase your personal visibility and/or to increase your business. This may lead you to believe that a campaign is self-serving—blowing your own horn. Well, that is what PR is all about.

The most efficient way to obtain this visibility is to draw up a plan of attack, a battle plan, a modus operandi. The industry uses such phrases as "draft a plan," "create a buzz," or "lay out a proposal."

We are taught in geometry that the shortest distance between two points is a straight line. Using this premise, a campaign defines the two points and devises the shortest distance between them for maximum efficiency in reaching one's goal.

Why have a campaign? Why not just take an idea and run with it, doing what comes naturally or instinctively, even impulsively? You can. And when you arrive at the end you may laugh, thinking you did it without formally preparing what you perceive as a "campaign." Well, understand this: the moment you stop to evaluate where you have been or where you are going, or to plan your next move, you are creating a campaign.

A campaign:

- defines a statement of purpose, a goal;
- saves time and effort in the long run;
- keeps the loose ends from falling off the page;
- creates a sense of order and avoids chaos.

A good campaign should not be rigid. It can and should be altered at any point along the way to fit the goal, rather than having the goal fit the campaign. If the nature of the goal involves others, one will always need to reevaluate. You cannot completely control what is not solely yours. Remember, any campaign that is not flexible will have great difficulty in succeeding as planned. Evaluating and adjusting the information you accrue daily is essential in the administration of a successful campaign.

A campaign can:

- be local, national, or international in scope;
- be directed at only one media outlet if it is the only appropriate placement, or it can be directed at many;
- include only print media, only electronic media, or a mixture of both;
- be designed only around suburban newspapers;
- be targeted only to syndications and wire services such as Associated Press (AP), United Press International (UPI), Newhouse, Knight Ridder, and Copley;
- include only local radio talk shows in the markets where your product has distribution;
- be instituted by one telephone call, one letter or one fax; by a targeted mass mailing; or by a blitzed mailing to all media.

Campaigns can involve three basic areas of media demographics:

1. Consumer media: magazines, newspapers, television, and radio programming targeted to the general public.
2. Trade media: business-to-business magazines, newspapers, etc.
3. Consumer-oriented trade media: media outlets targeted at specific consumer groups such as motorcycle enthusiasts, audiophiles, computer hackers, tennis buffs, etc.

Anatomy of a Campaign

Don Garrett used all three types of media for a client who manufactured caskets for pets. The primary focus of the campaign was to pet trade outlets. Consumer media might generate some orders, but targeted trade media would get him sizable orders from retail operations.

Usually, trade coverage is easy to get, but trade publications often have an unspoken policy of advertising in exchange for editorial coverage. In this case there was no advertising budget, making Garrett's primary focus difficult. So he re-directed his campaign first to obtain consumer coverage, hoping this would influence the trade publications to give him editorial coverage.

Garrett studied the consumer publications for a combination of credibility, demographics, topics, and circulation. He chose *People* magazine, with a circulation of over three million, as his target pitch, and he got it. He then took the story that appeared in *People* and had reprints made as part two of the campaign. He sent the reprints to the pet trade publications. And he hooked them, with little or no advertising requirements. Sales went through the roof. For part three of the campaign he made the reprint into a direct marketing piece targeted to every pet store chain and sizable independent store. "The more general the publication, the better my ammunition to merchandise to my target audience," says Garrett.

Note: As part of your campaign, put your banker on your mailing list. When you or your client need to extend your loan, it will make it a lot easier to do business with the bank, because they have been kept apprised of your business comings and goings through your media coverage.

Timing a Campaign

When planning time parameters, you must first define the time frame for completion of your goal. You may have long-range goals that last ten years or you may be planning an event next month. Second, you need to know media lead-time deadlines. For example, many magazines close Christmas stories in July. Third, you have to factor in time for setting up or producing materials. Assembling media kit materials can take up to six weeks, and depending on the size of the mailing list, creating the list can take weeks if you want the list to be as foolproof as possible.

A campaign can have several phases, plateaus, and multiple goals that can influence its length. For instance, if you have a product that has national distribution and you want to cover as many people as possible, using the least amount of energy and cost, the first phase should include:

1. appropriate syndicated columns
2. newspapers with a circulation of 100,000 and up
3. magazines with a circulation of over one million
4. national television talk and news shows
5. national radio talk and news shows

If that first phase doesn't get you sufficient coverage then the second phase should include:

1. newspapers with a circulation of 50,000 to 100,000

2. magazines with a circulation of under one million
3. local television and local radio

If coverage is still insufficient, then downscale again.

Imaging

Imaging is what Miss Mezzeppa was talking about. It is something you use to turn a typical person, place, or thing into one that is exciting, romantic, despicable, loyal, enchanting, etc. Imaging is powerful. Imaging produces instant identification and remains imprinted forever, whether consciously, unconsciously, or subconsciously. Imaging is the common ground that brings the campaign rhetoric down to the level of "everyman." Be careful of how you image something—it is very difficult to alter the mind's perception once you have introduced the image.

We can easily identify an image campaign for perfume or clothes or cars. But how does one image a grocery store into more than just a place to buy food? Stew Leonard's is quite an incredible grocery store in Norwalk, Connecticut. On special occasions he had people costumed as cows and chickens roaming through the store hugging, patting heads, and bounding up to customers with hors d'oeuvres, new brands, and sale items. His publicist, B. L. Ochman, suggested that if he increased the animals' appearance to an everyday occurrence, "shopping at his store would be like shopping at Disneyland." And the image was born.

Not only products or places are imaged. People also benefit from an image. Although the image may be in the form of what sounds like a nickname, it carries a great deal of impact because the image of the nickname sums up who and what they are. For example, publicist Dick Gersh arranged for *Time* to do a story on Casablanca Records' famous president, Neil Bogart, if Gersh could come up with an image. After watching his daughter enthusiastically chomping on her bubble gum to the rhythm of the music produced by Bogart's company, he coined the image "king of bubble gum music."

Publicist Jessica Josell developed the phrase "children are seen and Nat B. heard," for her client, director Nat B. Eisenberg, whom she imaged as "king of kiddie commercials." She also imaged award-winning jingle writer Steve Carmen, who has dominated the jingle industry for over twenty years with his thousands of recognizable jingles. It was when he came up with "Budweiser, the king of beers" that Jessica made him known as "king of the jingle jungle," and it has stuck to this day.

6

The Media Kit

"Fancy media kits are a waste. If you have a product with a very high end image, then maybe a fancy press kit will help, but only with the image. If the product is not good, the media kit won't matter."
—Michael Gelman, executive producer, "Live with Regis and Kathie Lee"

The media kit is a tangible stepping stone that provides the pertinent background on the people, places, and things involved with the project. It rounds out and backs up your request for media coverage. The media kit assists the media in translating the image into words. Media kits also provide a sales tool for the project. Although ultimately it is the idea itself that sells the project, the media kit can be a decisive feature in putting a marginal client over the top and strengthening an already strong campaign. If the media gets a messy, illogical, or incomplete kit, they have been known to decide against covering the project because of that kit.

Does a Fancy Kit Hold More Weight?

Noel Mishon opens the mail for the "Home Show." She acknowledges that if she saw a fancy media kit in the pile it would catch her eye, and she might pick it up to look at it, but after that it would go back in the pile to be taken to the appropriate researcher with all the others.

There is a point of diminishing returns. You want your kit to look professional, but many in the media think you are throwing money away if you try to do more. The bottom line is if the product is good, it sells itself.

Media Folders: To Cover or Not to Cover

You can staple the media kit contents, surround them with a rubber band, paper clip them, bind them, insert them in a plastic bag, or put them in a folder. Should you do the latter, you can print the cover, emboss it, cover it in velvet, make it glossy, and so on. It can be plain or designed, white or colored, stuck with doodads or lemon scented. To cover or not to cover is not the question; it is, to what degree is the cover done? That is the question.

If it is not important to the message of the campaign, then don't make a fuss. A folder will keep the contents together better than a paper clip will. If postage is a factor (and the cover is not important to the campaign) I suggest you pass on the cover. The most appropriate thing is that, inside, you provide what is needed and appropriate for your image and campaign. As long as you keep a clear relationship between need and service, need and product, or need and what is being provided, you will be successful in cover decisions. Don't let your ego or your need for your own visibility rule your decisions.

Always Put the Proper Identification on Each and Every Piece of Paper and Photo in the Media Kit

The premise here is simple. Accidents do happen and pages or pertinent information can easily be separated from the parent source. To avoid unclaimed, errant pages, always, and I repeat, always, have three forms of identification on every piece of paper that goes into the media kit or out of the office by messenger, mail, or fax:

1. company or subject identification

2. page number as it pertains to the total
3. responsible agent or contact person's name and telephone number

For example:

> Gourmet to Go (2 of 2)
> *Contact:* The Raleigh Group, Ltd.
> Raleigh Pinskey (212) 555-7144

Media Kit Components

There are standard components that go into making a media kit the sales tool that it is. The "anatomically correct" media kit should contain all of the following if available, but as in the principles of Zen, be in the moment and exercise your discretion. An in-depth description of each component follows this list.

Biographies or Project History
Stat or One Sheet
Photos
Company Project or Profile
Reprints of Articles
Minifeature

Optional:
Electronic or Print Media History List
Electronic media kit (EMK)

BIOGRAPHY OR PROJECT HISTORY

The purpose of a biography or project history is to inform, to provide background for the campaign pitch. It should be no more than two pages, double spaced. Try not to make it too dry, but don't bury the essence with cleverness. Strike a balance, stick to the point, and avoid using superlatives. Always be sure the spelling, grammar, and facts are checked carefully.

STAT OR ONE SHEET

The purpose of a *stat sheet* or *one sheet* is to give the project statistics or information regarding details in as concise a presentation as possible, without editorial comment. It is pure information. The *stat sheet* is used to list the performance of machinery, room dimensions, energy output, etc. *One sheets* are a basic outline of the information contained in a proposal, an article, a biography, etc.

PHOTOS

The photo should convey visually what you have written, whether it is a shot of a product, a personality, or a storefront.

- Photos should be black-and-white prints unless the newspaper or magazine takes color, in which case you should include slides, not prints. If the cost is prohibitive to include color slides, then mark very clearly on the release that color is available upon request.
- Photos should be eight by ten inches. Three-by-five-inch photos are acceptable, but not preferred, and could make the difference of being used.
- Make certain photos are not too dark for reprinting. You can use a copy machine to approximately determine how the picture will look when reprinted.
- Include both horizontal and vertical shots so you will be prepared for whatever space is available.
- Only head shots and product shots should be posed. The media prefer action shots where dancers are dancing, musicians playing, and golfers swinging. These provide a

better sales tool and one that's more interesting than traditional "grip and grin" shots. If you can, give the media a selection of stellar choices. Everyone likes to think that they don't have the same picture as their competition. Don't be insulted if they want to take their own pictures.

- Always caption or identify the subject of the picture and include a contact name and phone number. Put this information on a sticker on the back of your photos, or have the information printed or typed on the front in the margin.

Note: If you are using a folder, an unwritten law always puts photos on the left side of the media kit, unless the media kit is primarily pictures, in which case the right side is fine.

REPRINTS

Michael Gelman, producer of "Live with Regis and Kathie Lee," chuckles at how many times a client hasn't made it through the pitching maze of his show, even though they are interesting. And then they appear in *People* magazine or the *New York Times* and all of a sudden he takes notice. "Funny how being in another media gives them credibility."

Reprints show the media that you are credible in the eyes of another observer, especially if the journalist is considered an expert. Reprints affirm the viability of the client in the marketplace.

You should always try to have some reprints in a media kit. A few is plenty; too many and the media will look at them and say, no, the story's already been done.

- Choose the best and most recent articles. If it is over a year old, but the article is great placement, take off the date.

- Never switch the newspaper or magazine's name. It is simply unethical.
- Don't include trade reprints in a media kit you are sending to the consumer media, and don't send consumer reprints to the trade media. It's apples and oranges.
- It is considered unethical to delete negative comments from the reprint.

Many times I have found that no one likes to be the first to write about the client. So, even if it was in "The Toilet Paper Times," as B. L. Ochman refers to it, at least it was somewhere, and that gives it credibility. If you are dealing with a first-time client and there are no reprints, you can either mention the first-time status in the body of the pitch letter that accompanies the media kit, or you can wait for them to call and ask you if any exist. This is where knowing your media comes in. If you know they like being the first on something, you have that on your side. Again, be in the moment.

MINIFEATURES

The purpose of a minifeature, or *canned feature*, as it is sometimes called, is to offer smaller newspapers with staffing restraints a completed piece. Essentially, it is the extension of the two-page bio, and sometimes it will be used as is, but do not expect it to take the place of an interview. Many in the media are grateful for the canned feature because it helps them write a piece without having to do research beyond the media kit.

ELECTRONIC MEDIA HISTORY LIST

An electronic media history list is a chronological list of interviews the client has done on television and or radio. It establishes the necessary media credibility in a concrete manner and eliminates the need to send tapes until they are necessary.

ELECTRONIC MEDIA KITS

An Electronic Media Kit is a video taken of the spokesperson, product, or project. It is referred to as an EMK or an EPK, the P standing for press instead of media. Either is acceptable, but an EMK is more accurate and representative of its purpose.

An EMK can showcase the spokesperson, product, or project in an auditory/visual format; it can be used as a clip reel or as actual footage for a segment.

The EMK is a component of the written media kit, and comes with its own criteria.

When used as a *showcase*, the EMK should be between three and five minutes in length. It should provide valuable information about how the audience can benefit from the product. Carefully watch a well produced segment on television. Study how it is scripted, and duplicate the basics in your EMK.

When used as a *clip reel*, the EMK is comprised of snippets of your client's appearances on television. To make a clip reel, use two three-minute interviews and one six-minute interview and use the programs' lead-ins for enhanced credibility. It is important to present actual interviews to show how you or your client can handle the questions on-air. If you only have one interview, use a three-minute segment and a six-minute segment from the same interview. If you have done many interviews, list the others as part of a total media interview list in a directory at the end of the clip and in the media kit under Electronic Media History.

As for sending an EMK along with your press kit, don't, unless you have spoken with the media person directly, or checked on the department's policy about sending unsolicited tapes. Unsolicited tapes usually get filed in the "circular file." Even if money is no object, don't send it. Mark at the bottom of your pitch letter that you have an EMK available upon request, using it as a selling tool when you call to follow up. If you want the EMK returned, you must enclose a self-addressed stamped envelope and make it very clear on the letter, the envelope, and the cassette that you would like it returned.

Totally different than a clip reel, a *finished segment piece* containing three minutes of your agenda and two to three minutes of background information on you or the project will allow for the local stations to use your segment as an audio/visual representation, should you not be touring those markets. *This must be written and produced professionally*, on three quarter inch tape or one inch, prefaced with a directory, and cued to go. Have the contact information written on the case as well as the cassette.

Sending the Product Along With the Media Kit

Many media have rules against accepting unsolicited products and will send them by return mail for the simple reason that they can be misconstrued as gifts, and many media are not allowed to accept gifts. So check on the policy first before you go sending them. The rule of thumb of Andrew Sher of "Everyday" is to send a comprehensive media kit with good pictures using different angles, done in color and black and white so the product is adequately displayed. Polaroids will do. If the media's interest is piqued by the materials they will request a product showing. Even video tapes of the product are discouraged. This of course does not preclude you from sending it, it is just an insight into how they prefer to do business. If you think that they can't understand or believe how great the product is without seeing it, then by all means send it, but, as Michael Gelman advises his follow-up callers, "If you send out your products, don't expect to get them back. It's so crazy—half the time it doesn't get here, and once it's here it gets thrown onto a shelf, and things disappear."

Debby Supnick, of the "Home Show," feels that it's always nice to have something to show in the meeting, but it really isn't necessary. They've been at this a long time and can tell from a letter what you are talking about. A picture would be fine. And if they would like to know more they will call you.

As for sending food, because of product tampering and Halloween scares, the media are a little squeamish about what foods they accept from unknown sources.

How to Send Your Media Kit

Many in the media commented that when you send your media kit by UPS or Federal Express it comes at a different time than the mail, which means that if the person to whom it is addressed is there at delivery it might get a little more attention. To some it shows that you care a little more and have spent time, effort, and money to make sure it gets there, but after it's opened it goes in the pile with all the rest of the mail that has come in that day. The only genuine advantage to sending it that way is if you want a signature for your files, or if you want peace of mind. Actually, in many cases UPS surface is approximately the same cost as the regular mail, and you get a signature.

If you are sending many media kits to one area, and you want to be certain that they have been delivered without calling every place you sent them, you might want to call information and get the name of a messenger service in that area, or call an advertising agency or PR firm in that city and ask who they use. Then arrange to mail or messenger your individually wrapped materials in one package to the messenger service; they, in turn, can deliver the kits to all the media to which the kits are addressed.

7

Mailing Lists, the Backbone of Public Relations

"Steve Dunlevy, the metropolitan editor of the *New York Post*, hasn't been on staff for four years and yet he still gets at least twenty pieces of mail each day."

—Marianne Goldstein, assistant city desk editor, *New York Post*

Compiling a media mailing list is like baking a cake. You can make it from scratch by gathering the ingredients yourself, you can use a commercially prepared mix, you can use the mix as a base and add personal ingredients that help make the batter a bigger success, or you can go out and buy a cake and not get your hands dirty at all. With media mailing lists you can compile the data yourself; you can buy lists; you can buy a list, augmenting it with your own contacts; you can do business with a service that will take your media materials and do the job from start to finish—from data base compilation to printing to stuffing to sending (fax, messenger, mailing). Most PR company mailings employ various combinations of these approaches.

Did you know that:

- CNN interviews an average of 25 people on-air a day?
- There are 16,000 dailies and 5,800 weeklies, biweeklies,

and monthlies that cover the metropolitan, suburban, and rural American population? Publicists usually only mail to the top 300 newspapers, because some consider it a waste of time to mail to a newspaper with a circulation under 125,000.

- There are over 350 general interest magazines, and publicists only service approximately 50, or those with a circulation over 500,000, unless they are targeting a specific audience?

- There are 650 television station outlets and over 3,000 radio talk shows?

Contrary to popular belief, there is life beyond New York, Los Angeles, Dallas/Ft. Worth, Houston, Atlanta, Boston, San Francisco, Cleveland, Minneapolis/St. Paul, Washington, D.C., Baltimore, and Chicago. And many secondary and smaller markets yet would love to talk about your project if only they knew it existed!

When Mike Hughes was a producer at NBC television, he remembers that he would just take calls when he felt like it, only taking the crème de la crème and turning many people down even if they could have been marginal. Now, as publisher of *Publicity Express*, a magazine that promotes placements with TV and radio talk shows, he tells me that producers are on the other side of the coin and they are out at industry conventions looking for on-air guests. KGO, the ABC-owned and -operated and most dominant station in San Francisco, attends the American Booksellers Association convention looking for good guests. Why? National shows cover more people in one shot than in the traditional publicity tour. Producers don't have to traipse across the country for a fifteen- or thirty-day hectic existence when they can sit in comfort on the set of a single national show whose entire audience is made up of the very same listeners and viewers that would see them on countless local shows.

Television and radio are not the only media that are looking to fill space. Print has become a big consumer of soft news. With people getting their hard news in headline-like newscasts from television and radio, newspapers are relying more and more on their in-depth, soft news coverage to promote and keep readership interest.

Well, if there is such a need to fill the air time on radio and television talk shows as well as the space in newspapers and magazines, how does one get to them? Everyone knows about *People* and *Us* and "Oprah" and "Geraldo," but how do we get on "AM Cleveland" or "Good Morning, Detroit" or to Orlando, Florida, or even Scranton, Pennsylvania? And if you don't have the time or inclination to do it yourself, or an average of $3,000 a month plus expenses to hire a PR firm, does that mean you are out in the cold?

How are you going to know the players without a scorecard? How are you going to know which race the horse is in without a racing form? To whom are you going to send your media kits if you haven't compiled a mailing list?

A mailing list, or media list as it is sometimes called, contains no magic, no mystery. All you need is a little common sense. Essentially, the list contains the names, addresses, and phone numbers of the contacts in print, radio, and television that are pertinent to your project, and it is not very difficult to compile.

Compiling the Lists Yourself

The easiest way to compile a list is to call the particular media outlet and ask them to whom you address a story idea for your particular project. As with anything, there are nuances to the obvious, so I will attempt to give you a bit more information about approaching each media.

TELEVISION TALK SHOWS In all national, and many of the larger regional television shows, each show is divided into topic segments and usually has its own producer. The segment producer may be responsible for his own bookings—obtaining talent, the people who will be interviewed in a segment—or the segments may have a talent coordinator, sometimes called a booker or researcher, who decides what is the right talent for that topic segment. Ultimately, who will be on the show is decided by the executive producer, the person responsible for the overall image of the show.

It is appropriate that your mailing list should include the name of the executive producer, the particular segment producer for your project, and the talent coordinator-booker, should there be one for the topic.

Note: If time and manpower is limited, send it to the executive producer. When you call to follow up, he will direct you to the proper segment person.

If you feel you may have sent it to the improper person, or the person to whom you have addressed it no longer works there, calm down, all is not lost. Most staffers will see that the materials are passed on to the proper person. If not, you'll find out when you call to follow up (this will be discussed in length later under the topic of list maintenance). At a television show, where the internal structure is similar to what I have just described, all appropriate material is presented in a staff meeting presided over by the executive producer.

Do not send material to the host—it will end up in the fan mail. Do not send material to the experts (the person who does the medical update, covers gardening news on a weekly segment, etc.) or semiregulars, as they are sometimes called, before you check to see if they book their own guests or plan their own material. Usually the segment producer and the talent coordinator put this segment together with the expert only as on-camera talent.

Michael Gelman, executive producer of "Live with Regis and Kathie Lee," says, "Develop a relationship with someone on the staff with whom you do business, someone who will always know who you are when you call. If they ever use one of your ideas and it works out well they will be much more likely to take your call in the future. Although it is never prudent to put all of your eggs in one basket, in this case, if you are well respected by this one person, your name will get around—everyone knows what's going on in these offices."

If you have mailed to several producers and bookers at the same show, Mr. Gelman feels that you shouldn't pursue your follow-up individually with every one of the producers. If one turns you down, don't call another producer or booker on the same staff. Often that person will direct you to a more sympathetic ear, but if you have determined that the no is final, the staff of the show will hear about your shopping the other producers and you run the risk of being negatively labeled as overly aggressive or as a go-behind-the-back type. That won't do you any good.

Gelman also recommends, "Send your material to the executive producer as well. It doesn't hurt to do that, because everything must eventually go to the executive producer anyway, and if you send it there, you're ahead of the game."

Another way to learn the appropriate names and positions is to watch the crawl—the role call at the end of the show. Check the position and name that will best suit you or your project's needs.

TELEVISION NEWS   The assignment editor is the target person. He assigns the news crews and segment producers, or will pass your story on to experts if they are responsible for their own material. In order to cover all of the bases, ask for the name of the executive producer for each of the daily news shows, mailing your material to each of them.

RADIO TALK SHOWS   Depending on the size of the staff, radio talk shows are not much different than television talk shows. The talent coordinator or booker, the producer, and the host are all targets. If your postage budget will allow, send it to all three, if not, always send it to the producer. Check first, though, because in many shows, national and local, the host fills every role but that of the engineer.

RADIO NEWS   As in television news, the assignment editor is the target. But it never hurts to send it to the reporters, the producer, and the executive producer. There are night and day and weekend assignment editors. This can drive you crazy, so if you are not familiar enough with the system, just send it to the assignment editor and follow up later. Since releases get filed into a daily file, more often than not, your release will end up where it is supposed to.

MAGAZINES   Unless the publisher and executive editor are involved in the day-to-day editorial side, there is no reason to send it to them. Your targets are the managing editor, section editors, and staff reporters. The managing editor will pass it on to the appropriate section editor, but it is more direct (and will look more personal) if you call for the section editor's name and send it to him or her directly.

NEWSPAPERS   For dailies, the publisher and executive editor usually are not involved in the daily editorial operations. Your targets are the managing editor, city desk, listings editor, weekend section, columns, and the general editorial staff, which houses the section editors and staff reporters. If you can't figure out the proper target, send it to the managing editor.

Note: If they print a Sunday paper, the staff is different and all sections must be treated separately. With the weeklies and monthlies, the publisher is often the editor and even a good part of the editorial staff.

BE CAREFUL   Do not make the mistake of assuming continuity in the industry in regard to every department's function. If you are going to send without checking first, the best bet for each outlet is:

Television talk shows: send it ATTENTION Executive Producer

Television news: send it ATTENTION Assignment Editor

Radio Talk Shows: send it ATTENTION Producer

Radio news: send it ATTENTION Assignment Editor

Magazines: send it ATTENTION Editor

Newspapers: news: ATTENTION City Desk
                  events: ATTENTION Listings/Calendar Editor
                  features: ATTENTION Lifestyles Editor
                  products: ATTENTION New Products Editor

What Media Job Titles Mean

TV AND RADIO (ELECTRONIC MEDIA)

TRAFFICKER Some shows have a central person who logs in all mail. Even if you address your letter to a particular person, if it contains a pitch it is still kicked back to be logged in by the trafficker and then returned to the addressee.

RESEARCHER This title holds different meanings. For some media, it is the person who does the actual research on the segment. For some it is the fact checker and for others it is the same person as the booker.

BOOKER A booker receives the media kits and phone pitches, and if he decides that the subject matter is suitable for the show, it will be taken into the production meeting. Some shows allow each segment to have its own booker while others combine segments.

TALENT COORDINATOR On some shows this term is used interchangeably with booker. But for some shows it is used exclusively for the segments that have to do with entertainment personalities.

SEGMENT PRODUCER This is the person who makes the segment work. Based on the information obtained by the booker or talent coordinator, the segment producer is responsible for choreographing the actual segment. If there is no scriptwriter, then the segment producer will perform this function as well. He or she is responsible to the executive producer for the content of the final on-air piece.

PRODUCER This person is responsible for all the segments and answers to the executive producer. In radio it may be the only position between the reporter and the on-air personality.

This is the position that pulls it all together, the hub of the wheel, so to speak.

EXECUTIVE PRODUCER   This is the person who holds the vision together. All bookers, talent coordinators, segment producers, and producers report to this person. This is the final say for all ideas.

MAGAZINES AND NEWSPAPERS (PRINT)

PUBLISHER   This person is the equivalent to the TV and radio executive producer and usually makes the final decisions regarding editorial and advertising issues.

EXECUTIVE EDITOR   The person who oversees the daily operations, coordinating all departments and answering to the publisher.

MANAGING EDITOR   The daily manager of the editorial department.

EDITORS   Depending on the size of the magazine or newspaper, they may oversee all sections or departments or may have their own sections. Some magazines have Regional or West Coast or East Coast editors. In some cases they are really staff reporters, in others they are responsible for a staff.

REPORTERS   These are the foot soldiers. Publications differ in their assignment policies—some allow their reporters to suggest stories, others only assign through the assignment editor or section editor.

FREELANCERS   Sometimes called contributing editors, these are reporters and writers who are not on staff and usually contribute to various publications. They are usually listed as such on the masthead and you can send them query sheets as to their subject preference at the publication to which they contribute. Some staffed publications do not use them, others do even though they have a paid staff, and then there are those who rely only on freelancers for their editorial staff.

Note: If you are dealing with a company with East Coast, West Coast or Regional offices, determine the status of the office before you mail your materials. It is best to call the main office of the publication first. A regional office may simply be an advertising representative's office or the outpost of a regional editor who must report to the main office. Find out who makes the decisions and send it there.

BE CAREFUL: Don't make the mistake of paralleling the positions in the media.

- Don't make the mistake of assuming that the titles for each radio or television show, each magazine or newspaper have the same responsibilities as any other media outlet. There is often little industry consistency in media positions.

- Make your subject needs specific when asking for the responsible person. Ask the person to whom you are speaking what his job is. If you are speaking with a receptionist, a temp, a new employee, or a secretary who has only cursory knowledge of what you need, politely ask for someone in charge. There is usually a secretary or an overall office person who can be a more reliable source. If not, ask for the show's publicity person and explain your plight.

Why Keep Your Lists Updated?

"Hello, I'd like to speak with Ms. Stanton, the Health and Fitness editor." To which the receptionist politely replied, "No, you can't, she's dead." Trying to recover from my embarrassment I fumbled and asked him if this had happened recently. "No, over two years ago," he said politely. To get my foot out of my mouth, I countered with the information that I hadn't contacted his paper in over two years and was preparing an update. To which he responded, "Don't feel bad. We get mail for dead people all the time."

Categorically, the single most important part of everyone's media campaign is the accuracy of their lists.

The strong point of obtaining a list from the media directories is that they give you the broad picture—the media names, addresses, and phone numbers along with departmental information. Past that, I wouldn't trust them farther than I could throw them. Harsh words, you say? Words of wisdom, I say. Lists are obsolete the minute they are compiled. People move, change jobs, get fired, retire, and pass on. Media outlets go out of business, move, merge, and change their names, addresses, and phone numbers.

When talking to people in the media I was told ridiculous stories about mailings to people who hadn't worked there for years, to wrong departments, to names unbelievably misspelled. When I take on a new client, I insist upon seeing their mailing list as well as having the right to update it before anything with my company name goes out. On a recent client acquisition, I came across the name Mr. Daving Infusino. As I was about to put a question mark next to the name, I noticed it was the *San Diego Union*. Could it be? Mr. Daving Infusion was none other than Ms. Divina Infusino. Then I found Mr. Christian Wright. You got it. Ms. Christiana Wright. How about Mr. Alexander Anderson? I wonder if Alexandra's mother had any idea what her daughter would be up against, as does Charla Krupp's mother. Charla is constantly getting mail addressed to Charles.

Do those vast numbers of misspelled, misaddressed people have a sense of humor about this? I would have to say that a few did not mind. But the majority absolutely did mind. But not out of ego. The most common complaint was not that the pitch was not personally targeted to them or their publication, but that the sender's work was, well, sloppy.

Patty Neger of "Good Morning America" told me, "If you want me to take you seriously, know how to spell my name. If the idea is stupendous, a mistake like that doesn't stop me.

But if the idea is mediocre, and if it is someone I don't know, yes, it keeps me from going forward. If it is someone I know, and it has never happened with them before, I excuse that, once."

Eileen Daspin, formerly of *Fame* magazine, got people who would call with the column name from a different magazine. She politely told them no, that's the wrong magazine, and then she automatically has no interest in talking to that person. As she says, "It just puts me off."

"After all," says Rebecca Batties of VH-1 TV's International Division, "If you don't know the name, how can you play the game?"

The Source of Mistakes

The *New York Daily News* Health and Fashion editor Liz Rittersporn receives numerous calls and letters on a daily basis for Home Furnishing editor Liz Forgang. Even Ms. Rittersporn's voice mail identifies the fact that "if you want Liz Forgang, call extension ###." The culprit, she found from polling the callers, was an incorrectly compiled directory that was six years old. She figures that not in this lifetime will it be straightened out. People don't buy directories each year, and people pass lists on to their friends, who pass lists on to their friends, ad infinitum.

A logical question would be, instead of wondering if you are sending it to the proper person, what if you eliminate names and send it ATTENTION Assignment Editor, as you would do for television? The *New York Post*'s Marianne Goldstein told me, "Although I couldn't vouch for any other media, *there is no one with the designated title of assignment editor* at the *New York Post*!!! There are *sections* who have assignment editors, but there is no *overall* person that is in the job of trafficker. If such a piece of mail comes in addressed to Assignment Editor, it goes into a big pile on an empty desk that may be opened that day. Enter the person who has this desk at night. If he finds a pile of anything on what is at this point his desk, he will dump it. He doesn't care, he does not care! He figures it isn't his mail."

But what you can do is use the nonspecific identification plan: target a particular department. The Children's Video Editor may be assigned by the Arts and Entertainment editor, but if you didn't know that and labeled it ATTENTION Children's Video Editor, it has a better chance of finding the right person.

Gannett's Barbara Nachman is not in the least obsessed with getting mail that isn't pertinent because she likes to learn about things that are happening. And besides, even if it is a one in one-hundred chance that it will be a dynamite story, she wants to have that story. Maybe someone or something will catch her eye that may tie in with something she is writing or might write in the future.

Duplications and Multiple Mailings

Many of the media asked me why do they get two, three, or four copies of the same release. They resent the duplication of effort and cost. After opening two of the envelopes, the reaction is to stop and not open the agency's other envelopes, but they fear that if they throw them away there might be something different in them.

The mystery of the multiple mailings has to do with poor list maintenance. In Liz Rittersporn's case, perhaps she is on the health list, the fitness list, and the beauty list. Maybe she is listed under the *Daily News,* The *New York Daily News,* and *New York Daily News*. Maybe her name is misspelled and she comes up any number of times because of Rittersporn, Wittersporn, or Ritterspoon. In this day and age, with the available technology, it is generally unacceptable to have duplications.

Updating Your Lists the Easy Way

Quarterly list update queries are very helpful and painless. They are a wonderful way to gather information. Here's what to consider when designing an update:

- Make certain that you ask all the information you want to know. It should be designed to give you the who, what, where, and why of what you want to know. Read it over several times, with a break in between readings to give you time to see things differently.
- Use a No. 10 envelope and enclose a No. 9 envelope that has your return address either printed or done with an address stamp.
- Return postage is not necessary if you are sending to a company. It is considered doing business. If you are mailing to a freelance or bylines list, these people have to assume the cost, so it is courteous to stamp it, but not necessary.
- Make certain you include a line for the company or individual's name, otherwise you get back a query with no identifiable markings, which is a waste. Checking the postmark doesn't offer a clue as to who sent it.
- Keep it brief but inclusive, no more than one page.

Don't be afraid to put a qualifying statement saying, "If you don't return this query, your name will be removed from the list." If the media feel that it will benefit them in the long run, they will return it. I get 70 percent returns. In fact, when making follow-up calls, the media will apologize for not sending it back yet, wanting to know if it's too late?

Los Angeles Independent editor Brian Lewis told me he would gladly give up his sandwich time to fill in a questionnaire if it meant he could correct some of the mailing list horrors. *Pulse!*'s Brian Griffith would welcome query letters.

"Why not, it helps everybody. It may take a while, but I'll do it."
Even the *New York Times*'s Angela Dodson and the *New York Daily News*'s Liz Rittersporn said yes. When I asked, I would first get a squint, and half a frown. But the "no" headshake quickly turned to a yes as you could see them thinking of the possibilities of correct spellings and the possible elimination of misdirected mail. In fact, no one said no.

Sample update query:

TO: Arts and Entertainment Editor
RE: Request for Information
I would appreciate it if you could take the time to fill this in and return it. I have provided a self-addressed envelope for your convenience.
PLEASE IDENTIFY THE NAME OF YOUR MEDIA, SO WE CAN PROPERLY COMPUTE THE DATA (OR INCLUDE YOUR BUSINESS CARD):

_____

DO YOU REVIEW CHILDREN'S VIDEOS? YES __ NO __
DO YOU REVIEW CHILDREN'S AUDIOS? YES __ NO __
    PREFERENCE: AUDIOCASSETTE _____ CD _____
SEGMENT/COLUMN NAME: _____
FREQUENCY OF SEGMENT/COLUMN: _____
NAME OF REVIEWER FOR CHILDREN'S VIDEOS: _____
NAME OR REVIEWER FOR CHILDREN'S AUDIOS: _____
ADDRESS IF DIFFERENT THAN ENVELOPE:

_____

ARE YOU PLANNING ANY FEATURES ON CHILDREN'S VIDEOS AND/OR AUDIOS IN THE NEAR
FUTURE: YES _____ NO _____ DEADLINE? _____
ARE YOU PLANNING A CHRISTMAS GIFT COLUMN? __
WHEN IS YOUR DEADLINE? _____

THANK YOU FOR YOUR COOPERATION,
SURVEY MEDIA CONTACT:
    MS. RALEIGH PINSKEY (212) 555-7144

Commercial Media List Data Base Services

The mass media boom has birthed a plethora of services that plug you into the media, giving you outlets to promote everything from widgets to wombats, and from salads to sex.

Note: These services only guarantee that they will get it there—it is still up to you to follow through, to contact the editors and producers to give them a little nudge, a little sales pitch, a little sizzle. But at least the services give you a start.

Besides an extra hand, data base services offer the opportunity to broaden the scope of the project through media outlets that you probably never knew existed. It's like having your own employee whose job would be to monitor the talk show market for additions and cancellations, track personnel changes, stuff and mail your materials, produce, distribute, and track your electronic media kit, create, distribute and monitor your media release, and create and maintain your mailing lists. Quite an overall savings in time and effort! An integral part of the *Zen of Hype*!

Some services specialize in electronic media (radio and television), some participate in print only (newspapers and magazines), and some combine the outreach as a full-service company going to all media.

PR SERVICES FOR RADIO, TELEVISION TALK SHOWS, AND NEWS

RADIO-TV INTERVIEW REPORT is a *bimonthly* magazine that lists project pitches and profiles. It's mailed at no cost to the over 5,000 radio-TV talk show and TV news programming executives nationwide. The client pays a minimal fee to be included in this much utilized and well respected PR tool.

Contact: Radio-TV Interview Report, Bradley Communications Corp., 135 East Plumstead Avenue, Landsdowne, Pennsylvania 19050. (215) 259-1070.

PUBLICITY EXPRESS is a *monthly* magazine reaching 5,000 electronic media outlets, similar in intent to *Radio-TV Inter-*

view Report. This equally well respected tool also provides follow-up capabilities.

Contact: Publicity Express, 1563 Solano Avenue, No. 223, Berkeley, California 94707. (800) 541-2897.

MEDIA RELEASE SERVICES TO PRINT AND ELECTRONIC OUTLETS

If it has to be there today or tomorrow morning at the latest, and you don't have the fax numbers, computer terminal dedicated phone numbers, or the addresses to send mailgrams, how can you do it?

PR NEWSWIRE (PRN) is a *daily* service accessing the world's largest media telecommunications network through satellite, fax, mail, and database. PRN instantly delivers your news release and camera-ready photo transmissions to 1,000 newsrooms worldwide, coast to coast, regionally, or state by state. PRN specialty services include:

- Investors Research Wire provides distribution of financial news to more than 9,000 terminals in offices of brokerage firms, money managers, and institutional investors.
- Feature News Service guarantees early morning delivery of your feature story to more than 1,000 newsrooms, with a note to the editors that photos or other artwork are being transmitted by wire, or that photos and media kits are available upon request.
- Entertainment Circuit goes directly to hundreds of entertainment editors at newspapers and trades internationally and across the country with news about films, theater, music, dance, books, amusement parks, galleries, and a host of cultural events or other attractions.
- Photos by Wire satellite transmission service delivers your black-and-white or color photo immediately to selected newspapers nationwide, separately or coordinated with a release.

- Newsgrams combine overnight delivery and the impact of mail. They can target selected regions, states, or cities depending on the nature of the release.

Note: News releases sent out on PRN are retrievable from the leading databases—Dow Jones/Retrieval, NEXIS, Dialog, and many others.

Contact: PR Newswire, 150 East 38th Street, New York, New York 10155. (212) 832-9400. Outside New York: (800) 832-5522.

AUDIO FEATURES is a six-minute *daily* radio feed servicing 2,000 news and talk radio stations—stations with morning and evening news blocks, and all Associated Press (AP) and United Press International (UPI) audio feed wire service subscribers. Your written release is rewritten into "radio ready" format, scripted and recorded into a 60-second "news story," and sent directly into the newsrooms via AP and UPI audio lines.

Contact: Audio TV Features, 149 Madison Avenue, No. 804, New York, New York 10016. (212) 889-1342.

NORTH AMERICAN PRECIS SYNDICATE, INC. (NAP) is a *monthly* distributor of multimedia script and slide packages to radio and television news and talk shows by mail.

To radio: NAP mails timed 30- to 60-second scripts to 3,000 radio stations that have talk shows and news shows or news inserts between regular programming. (These are scripts, not "radio ready" cassettes.)

To television: NAP distributes four-color slides with 30- to 60-second scripts mailed to 325 independent or affiliate VHF stations and local cable broadcasters with talk and news shows. They do not service cable stations.

Contact: North American Precis Syndicate, Inc., 4209 Vantage Avenue, Studio City, California 91604. (818) 761-8400.

DERUS MEDIA is a *monthly* distributor of multimedia script and slide packages.

To radio: DM services 11,000 radio stations in their media bank. This includes 9,645 AM and FM stations, 630 college, 330 religious, 220 black, and 200 Hispanic stations.

To television: They mail four-color slide scripts to 1,000

outlets. Cable stations and networks are canvassed by a letter to determine which are interested in your electronic media kit. A reply card is enclosed if the outlet is interested, saving the client cost and materials (they will service your electronic media kits to the networks in the same fashion).

Note: They are the only service to offer a full-service division for the Hispanic market, including rewriting your materials in Spanish to assure language accuracy.

Contact: Derus Media, 500 North Dearborn, No. 516, Chicago, Illinois 60610. (312) 644-4360.

VIDEO NEWS CLIPS OR ELECTRONIC MEDIA KITS

Audio Features (see above) also makes video news clips, also known as electronic media kits. I have singled out Audio Features because of their unique method of distribution on their daily Associated Press and United Press International wire service feed which goes to 600 stations via satellite, or with exclusives to particular stations and networks, and PRN because of their vast communication network and specialized service data base that enhances pickup and awareness capabilities.

There are many other electronic media kit and video news clip production services that can provide satellite rental time. To find them, look in your local telephone directory, call a local PR company or your local newsroom. The newsroom will be able to tell you who provides the best service.

Contact: Audio TV Features, 149 Madison Avenue, No. 804, New York, New York, 10016. (212) 889-1342.

Contact: PR Newswire, 150 East 38th Street, New York, New York 10155. (212) 832-9400. Outside New York: (800) 832-5522.

PR SERVICES FOR THE PRINT MARKET

Feature placement services provide the print media with camera-ready editorial and captioned photos. Up until the

1970s they were known as "mat services" because they used a cardboard matrix process with the copy prepared on cardboard or fiber mats into which they poured lead to make the print molds. They no longer use mats, having spent considerable expense updating their systems to offset, disc, and computer. With the new technology, a new image and a new preference has come to be addressed as "feature placement services."

These *monthly distributors* of camera-ready releases provide the ability to saturate the secondary markets without the big bucks investment. These are papers most likely to use camera-ready releases about people, places, and products which are not local or community-related stories. Magazines are not included in the distribution because most magazines do not accept camera-ready art for feature stories. Many prefer to take their own pictures. You are already familiar with two of them, North American Precis Syndicate, Inc. and Derus Media. The others are as follows.

NEWS USA INC.   distributes media release and editorial feature camera-ready art in a monthly package by mail, discs, and computer-to-computer on-line hookups to 10,000 newspapers. They also provides an Editor's Service Bureau daily interfacing with the top 100 dailies. They offer a twenty-four-hour electronic bulletin board providing the subscriber with a category menu of all previous releases.

Note: They are the only service that will guarantee you one hundred placements per feature, or they will run your release again at no charge.

Contact: News USA Inc., 2300 Clarendon Boulevard, Arlington, Virginia 22201. (800) 868-6872.

NORTH AMERICAN PRECIS SYNDICATE, INC.   specializes in servicing editorial and camera-ready art to suburban papers with a circulation under 40,000, which breaks down to 2,800 weeklies and 1,000 dailies with a total distribution of 3,800 newspapers.

Contact: North American Precis Syndicate, Inc., 4209 Vantage Avenue, Studio City, California 91604. (818) 761-8400.

DERUS MEDIA   is the only one of the four placement services whose package is not ruled by a monthly deadline; rather, they go out when the release has been approved by the client. Quarterly, the entire release package for those three months is re-sent to all 8,000 papers whether you bought the top or the bottom menu. Editors will be able to reconsider your release again if they passed on it already, or if they have never seen it.

Note: They do not service the top 350 newspapers, those with a circulation of 75,000 and up.

- They offer a three-level distribution menu: 1. all 8,000 newspapers, 2. a metropolitan package to the top 50 markets totaling 3,600 circulation, and 3. the top 2,500 newspapers.
- They will target your mailing to your needs by zip code, congressional district, rural or metropolitan, top 100 cities, etc.

Note: At this time they are the only service of the four that will do this.

- They are the only service with a complete Hispanic database. They will rewrite, not translate, your release into Spanish.

Contact: Derus Media, 500 North Dearborn, No. 516, Chicago, Illinois 60610. (312) 644-4360.

METRO PUBLICITY SERVICE   mails to 7,000 newspapers with a potential distribution of 80 million readers. Their monthly package differs from the other services by using *theme sections* twenty-two times each year, featuring subject matter from gifts to gardens, furnishings to fashion, and targeting holiday and seasonal merchandise. Other feature packages include:

- Prime Cuts is for featuring food, drink, kitchen appliances, and ideas for entertaining.
- Timely Features is dated material lending itself to a series of continuing columns or monthly byline articles.

- Custom Sections is for highlighting multiproduct lines, new product introduction, special events, or promotions.
- Minisections are additions to the regular theme sections of particular consumer interest such as the Environment, the Senior Scene, Children's Corner. They will work with you to design your own.

Contact: Metro Publicity Services, 33 West 34th Street, New York, New York 10001. (212) 947-5100.

MEDIA BANKS: OUT-OF-HOUSE MAILING OPTIONS

If you want someone else to do the list research, stamp, stuff, and mail your material, companies such as Media Distribution, Bacon's Distribution, PR Newswire's U.S. Mail Service, and Burrelle's will mail your release to their data base of trade and consumer print and electronic outlets.

Media Bank Categories:

Trade Press	General Business Media
Consumer Magazines	Daily Newspapers
Weekly Newspapers	Television Stations
Radio Stations	Special Media Lists
News Services	Syndicates
Wire Services	Syndicated Business Columns
Syndicated Food Columns	Newspaper Sunday Supplements
Black and Hispanic Press	

Media Banks provide multilevel services such as:

Mailing	Product Mailings
Media Kit Assembly	Photo Reproduction
Printing	Letters
List Maintenance	List Consultation
Media Lists on Labels	Fax Service

Check to make sure that the category you select is complete and can meet your needs. Don't assume the list is all-inclusive.

Use some of your own contact names to test their list. *Ask questions!* The daily papers and electronic media newsrooms are their most complete lists.

Contact: Media Distribution Services, MDS/PRA Group, 1801 South Hill Street, Los Angeles, California 90015. (213) 749-7383.

Contact: Bacon's Media Information Systems, 332 South Michigan Avenue, Chicago, Illinois 60604. (312) 922-2400. Outside Illinois: (800) 621-0561.

Contact: PR Newswire, 150 East 38th Street, New York, New York 10155. (212) 832-9400. Outside New York: (800) 832-5522.

Contact: Burrelle's Media Information Systems, 75 East Northfield Road, Livingston, New Jersey 07039. (800) 631-1160.

NATIONAL MEDIA DIRECTORIES

Note: Check your local library before you go out and buy these directories. You can buy the data base list information on labels and disks without buying the bound hard copy.

There are several companies that provide directories for media outlets. The inherent problem is that contact names change even before the directory is printed. If you are concerned about accuracy, the names must be checked. Another pitfall lies with the national, all-inclusive directory-specialized categories. They are grossly incomplete. I checked the city and state category of a so-called leader in the field. I had more names on my personal list than what they gave me. The directory information is good for a starting point, but shouldn't be taken as gospel.

There are five companies that provide national media directories in bound printed reports, on computer disks, and on labels. Each provides a substantial data base of print, radio, network, and cable TV publicity outlets, including specific programming and editorial page information, demographics, and formats. The five are:

Contact: Bacon's Publicity Checker: Bacon's Media Information Systems, 332 South Michigan Avenue, Chicago, Illinois 60604. (312) 922-2400. Outside Illinois: (800) 621-0561.

Contact: BPI: BPI Media Services, 1515 Broadway, New York, New York, 10036. (212) 536-5263. Outside New York: (800) 284-4915.

Contact: Burrelle's Media Information Systems, 75 East Northfield Road, Livingston, New Jersey, 07039. (800) 631-1160.

Contact: Morgan-Rand, 2200 Sansom Street, Philadelphia, Pennsylvania 19103. (215) 557-8200.

Contact: Talk Show Selects, Broadcast Interview Source, 2233 Wisconsin Avenue, N.W., No. 406, Washington, D.C. 20007-4104. (202) 333-4904.

Exclusive to Morgan-Rand Publishing is a Feature News directory of "soft news" pages—food, family, fashion, etc. BPI (Billboard Publishing, Inc.) has a directory of Syndicated Columnists and News Bureau Contacts—listings of publications and wire services that provide local, regional, or nationwide bureau services. Unusual to the industry, BPI also provides you with monthly updates and edit search updates should you want to check the accuracy of a contact before you mail.

TALK SHOW "SELECTS"   is a very good directory with selective listings of the 640 most worthwhile and influential talk shows, hosts, producers, and program directors on the air, designed to maximize the efficiency of your media outreach programs. Only regularly scheduled shows that welcome outside sources are included by both state and major market.

Contact: Talk Show Selects, Broadcast Interview Source, 2233 Wisconsin Avenue N.W., No. 406, Washington, D.C. 20007-4104. (202) 333-4904.

POWER MEDIA "SELECTS,"   from the same people, identifies more than 3,700 of the most influential print and media contacts including newswires, syndicates, syndicated columnists, local and national newspapers, magazines, newsletters, and TV and radio talk programs. Organized into two sections, by both media category and type of news covered, each listing provides contact names and titles, publication, column or program name, phone number, street address, fax number, and detailed editorial rosters when available.

Contact: Power Media Selects, Broadcast Interview Source, 2233 Wisconsin Avenue N.W., No. 406, Washington, D.C. 20007-4104. (202) 333-4904.

LOCAL AND REGIONAL MEDIA DIRECTORIES

The Intercom Group, the Bulldog Reporter Newsletter people, puts out *Eastern* and *Western Media Contacts* indexed by state. Another necessity in your personal directory library is *New York Publicity Outlets*, which also publishes *Metro California*. Both are comprehensive, well-compiled directories.

Both companies' directories cover all the major and secondary media, with the Intercom Group adding newsletters. If you are working market by market, these directories must be considered bibles for your media needs.

As for other single-market directories, more and more are cropping up every day. To find them, you can call the library reference service where they will access *Books in Print* (see below) or you can call operator information in the area you need, request the number of a PR, agency and query them as to the existence of a regional, state, or local directory.

INTERNATIONAL MEDIA DIRECTORIES

Ulrich's International Periodicals Directory is an incredible reference source that includes periodicals, newsletters, magazines, and newspapers throughout the world by subject heading. *Contact:* Bowker Publishing, 121 Chanlon Road, New Providence, New Jersey 07974. (908) 665-2840.

COLLEGE MEDIA DIRECTORIES

American Passage Media Service's primary function is to place advertising in the college marketplace. Their rate card directory is helpful with major market college media information. They will print mailing labels for you of more than twelve hundred colleges by circulation demographics.

Contact: American Passage Media Services, 215 West Harrison Street, Seattle, Washington 98119. (206) 282-8111.

DIRECTORIES OF DIRECTORIES

With these directories, you needn't call around to the various directory companies.

Contact: Directory of Directory Publishers, Morgan-Rand, 220 Sansom Street, Philadelphia, Pennsylvania 19103. (215) 557-8200.

Contact: Directories in Print, Gale Research, 835 Penobscot Building, Detroit, Michigan 48226. (313) 961-2242.

The ultimate source of all printed books is *Books in Print* (use the subject guide). This list includes the publishing houses' current and past releases that are currently in print.

Note: All of the directory companies listed throughout the book (except Broadcast Media Source) have a comprehensive directory business providing directories in many categories other than media that could be helpful in many publicity campaigns.

NEWSLETTERS

There are two weekly newsletters which are invaluable tools: *Partyline, The Weekly Roundup of Media Placement Opportunities*, and *Contacts, The Media Pipeline for Public Relations People*. They list the new columns, shows, magazines, segments, etc. and what they are looking for. They report on freelance project needs and provide address and staff changes, spotlighting a media outlet and its editorial and personnel makeup.

And then there is the *Bulldog Reporter*. A very expensive newsletter with an Eastern and Western Edition. If you want a national scope, you have to subscribe to both. Primarily, it contains PR industry news, reporting on campaigns, job changes, and campaign signings. A biweekly, it does include a spotlight on a major media.

Contact: Bulldog Reporter, 2115 Fourth Street, Berkeley, California 94710. (800) 327-9893.

Contact: Contacts, 35-20 Broadway, Astoria, New York 11106. (718) 721-0508.

Contact: Partyline, 35 Sutton Place, New York, New York 10022. (212) 755-3487.

NEWSPAPER

Talkers, the Information-Radio Newspaper, is filled with insights and information on talk show personalities and programming news. "Hot Sources" is both a column and a listing service for spokespersons, complete with topics and contact numbers.

Contact: Talkers, Goodphone Communications, Inc., Box 60781, Longmeadow, Massachussetts 01116-0781. (413) 567-3189.

Note: The Overall PR Reference Source for assistance in the field of PR is the Public Relations Society of America (PRSA). Located in New York City, it is a vital professional resource, available to members and nonmembers alike. Besides their complete bibliography of public relations books, periodicals, and directories, they maintain a comprehensive library from which they can provide you with campaign and marketing ideas to help develop your public relations programs. They have more than one thousand PR subject files, information about people in the media, background facts on companies and organizations, and public relations case studies.

Contact: Public Relations Society of America (PRSA), 33 Irving Place, New York, New York 10003. (212) 995-2230.

8

Pitching Your
Project to the Media

"In this world of ours, it's all on how you can sell it. Then it doesn't matter if you end up telling them the same thing that everyone else has told them, because you've sold the sizzle."
—Michael Gelman, executive producer, "Live With Regis and Kathie Lee"

The pitch is your sales talk, your trumpet. The pitch lets them know you are coming. There are several ways in which you can alert the media to the fact that you have something happening or that you have something to say. And for each of the different media there is a special format that one must follow to maximize the type of exposure you are seeking.

- A Media Release conveys to the media basic information that they can release to the public or the trade.
- A Calendar Release uses the media to tell the public to mark a date on their calendars.
- A Camera Opportunity tells the media to bring their cameras because you have a picture for them to take.
- A Media Alert tells the media that something is happening and that they should attend.
- A Pitch Letter provokes the media to interview a subject.

Media Release

A Media Release is not an invitation to an event. The purpose of a Media Release is to inform the media of past, present, or future information about an event or project. You send a Media Release (sometimes called a News Release) when you want editorial coverage of the exact information you are sending. This may be on the election of officers, the opening of a new store in the mall, the receipt of a grant by a university, the installation of new equipment at a hospital, or the addition of a line of fragrance for a drugstore chain. Keep it straight, to the point, and don't exaggerate.

Media Releases are written in an editorial style that includes both a headline and body.

THE HEADLINE

Headlines are the most important part of a release. The headline can mean the difference between getting the rest of the release read or tossed. If the headline doesn't interest the media, they may never read the rest of the release. Headline motto to remember: "Make history or be history."

Newsrooms especially are besieged with hundreds of requests for media coverage each day. *Make it sizzle*. Headlines hold a great deal of power because they can make or break a campaign.

Headlines should be in bold type, capital letters, underlined, and double spaced. Headlines can be funny or tongue-in-cheek, but not obscure. The media are looking for facts in the headline. If the headline is obscure they will naturally presume that the release is obscure. Unless the reader understands the obscurity, you've lost him. The information given in the headline is the premise of the release in no more than a phrase or brief sentence.

THE BODY OF THE MEDIA RELEASE

Yes, there is life after the headline, but not a long one. In order to catch and keep their attention, the rule of thumb is to keep the text of the release to three or four paragraphs or two hundred fifty words, whichever comes first. Yes, it is possible to say what you need in that length because you have proven that you could say it in the headline! It should be double spaced, leaving room for people in the media to edit your copy to their needs.

FIRST PARAGRAPH Use your strongest bit of information without sensationalizing it. This first paragraph should embellish the headline. This is where you tell them the exact information you want them to know. The basic who, what, where, when, and why.

SECOND AND THIRD PARAGRAPHS You may not need these two paragraphs, but if you do, these need to answer two questions: Why I am sending this release? Why should you bother to read it?

FOURTH PARAGRAPH The fourth paragraph should give whatever background is necessary, briefly.

There is no sign-off or wrap-up in a Media Release, because with a Media Release it is understood that you are not asking them to do anything beyond printing the informational contents of the release.

CLIENT QUOTES The third or fourth paragraph may instead be a brief quote from a principal involved in the project. The quote is usually a commentary on the project. Quotes are appreciated by some media and rejected by others. Those who reject using the prepackaged quote would prefer to ask the principal for a response to a question of their own choosing. But you can't call each individual media and ask them if they want a quote, so I include the quote anyway, because it usually contains exactly what the client sees as the controlling purpose of the project. If I know the particular media person who will get this release doesn't appreciate prepackaged quotes, then I paraphrase it or just change the pronouns to make it fit.

HIGHLIGHT ESSENTIAL POINTS

Using a yellow or pink highlighting marker, go over the important words or points so the reader can glance down the release reading only the highlighted words or phrases. Many people in the media do this for themselves to help them talk from the release in the production meeting, so why not do it for them first? Of course, this is optional.

PERSONALIZING MEDIA ALERTS, CAMERA OPPORTUNITIES, AND MEDIA RELEASES

These are the same printed pieces of paper that will be sent to all the media—they carry no personalized touch. If I know the person at the photo or media desk, I put a Post-it with a personal one-line note and sign it, or write FYI (for your information) and a note saying, "I thought this would be of particular interest to you," or "Hope you can cover this," or "I hope you and the kids are well." It's a courteous gesture I use for those who I know care about the personalized touch.

Calendar Release, Bulletin Board Release, and Listings Release

Local television, radio, and print media all have community bulletin boards or calendars that will list your meeting, lecture, fair, hike, etc. Listings are part of editorial, not advertising! I found that a common complaint from the media was that people call in to list their event saying, "I'd like to place a free ad in the paper," or "I'd like to advertise my event." The calendar listing is an editorial function and an ad is an advertising function. The proper language is, "I would like to *list* my event." Otherwise, you may just get a bill for your "ad."

Sample Media Release:

```
CONTACT: DEE VYNE (213) 939-4477

March 25, 1990 FOR IMMEDIATE RELEASE:

STOLI UNDERWRITES 1990 "WORLD MUSIC SERIES"

    "WORLD MUSIC SERIES", a ninety-minute, live,
syndicated radio series designed for progressive
adult/contemporary jazz formatted radio stations
announces that STOLI has signed on as entertain-
ment sponser for the 1990 season.

    The series will be delivered on 15kHz on
Westar 4 and in digital stereo on Satcom 1-R to
150 stations for the continental United States,
internationally over Voice of America with a
listener reach of 130 million plus people weekly
in forty-four languages. Offered to stations on a
free basis, availabilities exist for noncompetitive
sponsers.

    "The two-year-old, highly successful show
grows from one to six live concert dates and will
be sequenced around major holiday weekends, kicking
off with Memorial Day," offers Sam Kopper, Director
of Operations. "We conceived of this ambitious
venture to allow for the progressive adult/contempor-
ary jazz stations to have something to offer their
audience on these highly 'special'ized weekends.

                        1 of 2
```

```
Stoli World Music Series

Page 2 of 2

CONTACT: DEE VYNE (213) 939-4477

Talents will be drawn from international, chartered
artists, in keeping with the design of STOLI's
vision for a cultural exchange. Their concept is
that music, like the product itself, knows no language
barrier."

    Production and distribution of the series is
provided by Sam Kopper/Starfleet Communications for
Peer Pressure Promotion, a division of Roger Lifeset,
Inc. For sales information call THE WORLD MUSIC
SERIES at (818) 370-9460. For station information,
call Peer Pressure Production at (818) 991-7668.

                        2 of 2
```

One hundred percent of the listings editors felt that the public doesn't know that the editors are your allies and not your enemies, that the paper is not fooling when they invite you to send in information about an upcoming event. Contrary to popular belief, no one is dressed as the grim reaper standing at the mail shot, cackling sinisterly, maliciously diverting the mail into a huge black sack marked "Next Galaxy." Here are the real reasons why your mail may not make it to the calendar:

- It is over one page.
- Any part of the basic who, what, where, when, why, and contact name and number is missing or incorrect.
- Too many spelling errors.
- You missed the deadline.

"54 Hours," the listing for the *Los Angeles Times*, announces at the finish of the column:

"INFORMATION TO BE CONSIDERED FOR THIS COLUMN SHOULD BE RECEIVED AT THE TIMES AT LEAST THREE WEEKS BEFORE THE EVENT. DO NOT TELEPHONE. MAIL ITEMS OF GENERAL INTEREST TO LAURIE SCHENDEN, 54 HOURS, THE TIMES, TIMES MIRROR SQUARE, LOS ANGELES 90053."

Newspaper pages have scheduled days and times when they must lock up, and no amount of begging can change that. When someone tells you they are on deadline for the information and they need it *now*, they mean it. Usually "soft news" pages close long before the "hard news." As a cost issue, you cannot keep all of the pages open until the last minute and then rush to close them all at once. This would require extra staff or overtime. So they systematically close pages. If you don't make that cut with your information, forget it.

If you are racing the deadline clock, don't assume that because you send a fax that it got to them on time for deadline. Not every department has a fax machine, and the person assigned to collect and deliver may have more to do than fax duty. It can lay there for hours before the proper person gets it. *Plan ahead, way ahead.* Events are not born overnight for the following day, and the Listings Editor knows this. The editor is well equipped with a file for upcoming events as far away as a year in advance.

Many cities have private listing services that sell daybook-event information to urban and suburban media, but you don't have to pay to list your event. Although subscribers usually include the major papers, radio and TV stations, and, occasionally, magazines, the bulk of the subscribers are suburban dailies, weeklies, monthlies, pennysavers, and mall papers, as well as the local suburban radio and TV stations. This distribution is called "mall & all." Check with suburban papers if such a service exists in your area and make certain they are on your mailing list.

If your city has a wire service bureau, send them a Media Alert-Camera Opportunity. They will place it in their daybook as well as send it out to the subscribers in their coverage radius.

BASIC CALENDAR LISTING FORMAT

- Identify the fact that it is a LISTING in the upper left hand corner. That way they are certain it is for that department.
- Date the release. If you send an update, they can identify which is the most current.
- Under the date, include the sender's name and phone number in case the media have questions and have the time to call. This can be different than the contact name and number in the body of the listing, which is usually the place for specific information about the event.
- Include a brief one- or two-sentence description of the event after the basic who, what, where, when, and why. Some calendars include this information.

Sample calendar listing/bulletin board release/listings release:

CALENDAR OR LISTINGS EDITOR
OCTOBER 10, 1990 FOR IMMEDIATE RELEASE
CONTACT: Dee Vyne, (213) 555-7741

WHO: Los Angeles Chapter of Songwriters Showcase
WHAT: CASSETTE ROULETTE AND PITCH-A-THON™
WHERE: Acapulco Restaurant, 7038 Sunset Avenue, Hollywood, ½ blk east of La Brea, south side of street, free parking lot on property (213) 469-5131
WHEN: 7 PM to Midnight
WHY: Los Angeles Songwriter's Showcase-produced, BMI-sponsored, giving amateur and semi-amateur songwriters a chance to have their taped songs heard by industry representatives. Per Tape Entry Fee: Members: $8/Nonmembers $10
For Information, Call: LASS, Len Chandler, (213) 555-1665

BACKGROUND: LOS ANGELES SONGWRITER SHOWCASE (LASS) HAS BEEN HOLDING THESE WEDNESDAY NIGHT SHOWCASES FOR 19 YEARS—OVER 1,000 WEDNESDAYS. Alumni include Stephen Bishop, Stevie Nicks, R. C. Bannon, Oingo Boino, Lindsey Buckingham, Robbie Neville, and more. Famous songwriters Diane Warren, Allan Rich, Michael Jay.

• Include one paragraph about the background of the event or organization. If there are space considerations for the column, and the editors make decisions based on reader interest, that background paragraph may make the difference between your event being an interesting one for their public and not being included at all.

• A # or several *** at the bottom of the page alerts the

reader that there is no other page and that you are finished.

- You don't have to use the WHO:, WHAT:, WHERE:, WHEN:, and WHY: in the margins, but they do provide a highlighting effect for the editor.

Camera Opportunity and Media Alert

The information and format of a Camera Opportunity and a Media Alert are exactly the same as the Calendar Listing. The only difference is to which media it is directed. Going back to our definition of a Media Alert: alerting the media there is something happening; a Camera Opportunity: alerting the media to come and bring their cameras. A Media Alert and a Camera Opportunity are directed to the media and ask the media to come and cover the event—a sort of show and tell. (A Calendar Listing is sent to the media but directed to the public.)

Headline the information with both Media Alert and Camera Opportunity. In most print cases the same editor assigns both the photographer and the reporter. As for TV, the Photo Opportunity is still accepted, but they prefer the phrase Camera Opportunity, which covers both the still and moving image.

For TV and radio coverage, you address it to the Assignment Editor who checks the release to see if it is appropriate for their media. If accepted, they file it by event date in a monthly folder. Reporter assignments are usually made one to two days in advance of the event.

For newspaper coverage, it's the City Desk. City Editors list your event in the *assignment book, daybook,* or *daily budget,* a compilation of all the department's assignment requests for the day so the person in charge will know who is available and who has already been assigned. Don't be afraid to call your local newspaper as to their assignment procedure. They would rather you get it right.

National magazines don't list or cover local events unless these events are at least national in interest. If you want a magazine to write a story on the client or organization sponsoring the event, call the magazine requesting the name of who may be interested in such a story or covers those story ideas.

Note: Do not rely on a Calendar Listings editor passing your release to the Assignment Editor or City Desk. Do not rely on reporters reading the Calendar Listings and asking to cover your event. Send appropriate releases to the appropriate people.

ADDITIONAL MEDIA RELEASE TARGETS

- Notify the private calendar newsletters. Not every community has them, but they are appearing more and more in medium to large cities. They are either mailed or faxed to media subscribers as well as PR agencies and organizations who can keep their eyes on creativity and planning.
- Notify independent TV crews that sell their feed to the stations.
- Notify the local wire service bureaus.

ALERT THE NEWSPAPER PHOTO DESK ABOUT YOUR EVENT

Although the Photo Desk does read the news desk's daybook, they also have one of their own. So, send a separate announcement to the Photo Desk of every newspaper, just in case the Editorial Desk doesn't get it or doesn't pass it on.

Interestingly enough, a newspaper's photo desk is more likely to dispatch a photographer to cover your event than the print Assignment Editor is to assign a reporter. In order to maximize coverage, events should be staged not only for editorial coverage, but also for camera coverage. Don't forget to leave them with the idea that you are having more than just a ho-hum person giving a speech, that there will be angry mothers and children with placards who are tired of being kicked out of their homes. Or that there will be people dressed as lettuce, radishes, and broccoli hugging customers and giving out vegetarian recipes at the American Heart Association exhibit booth.

If the photo desk assigns someone, don't insist upon milking the assignment desk for a feature. Rejoice. Although it means they didn't find that your event justified an entire article, they found it could be a "crowd pleaser" through visual representation. And at least you have the possibility of ending up with some coverage (a captioned photo in the newspaper) as opposed to no coverage at all. Besides, you know the old saying, "A picture is worth a thousand words"! A picture also makes a valuable reprint for the media kit.

Inform the Media of Any Attendance Restrictions

Once your event goes out on the wire or subscriber service, or is listed in the media calendars, it goes to all the media. If you have established media attendance restrictions or dress codes, be up front about it. Specify this in no uncertain terms. For example: If your event is a benefit, note if the media are expected to pay, if no photographers will be allowed or if there are photo restrictions; and, if there is a dress code, note that media will not be admitted unless appropriately attired.

A good PR person heads off a disaster before it begins. Alerting the media to restrictions ahead of time will definitely increase your PR quotient.

The Media Alert/Camera Opportunity, the Media Release, and the Calendar Listing are all tools to get your event noticed and, you hope, mentioned. But better than a mention is a feature. None of these release formats is appropriate in approaching the media about running a print feature or an electronic segment. These have a format all their own and it is called a Pitch Letter.

Pitch Letters

The pitch isn't the steak; it's the sizzle that will make your steak sound better than the next steak on the grill. It's the edge, the spin that makes you different from everyone else. It adds the shape and the color. It also conveys uniqueness and gets the media to respond, "I didn't know that!" or "Wow!" or "Now, that's interesting!"

A good Pitch Letter briefly explains what you have to offer and why the media should want it.

For example: Your client is twenty-one years old. He has a greeting card company whose humorous messages and delightful characters have won him many awards in his first year of business. But all this seems to lack sizzle. Shape the realism, add some natural color, show the media how the segment or the story can turn into an audience payoff for them. For TV, pitch the producer on having several of your client company's artists and copywriters on the show, having the audience suggest the mood or occasion for the card, and have the copywriters and artists create the card right there. Perhaps the creation can be added to the seasonal collection. Perhaps the proceeds from that card could go to the show's favorite charity. For the print media, you could do the same creativity in the offices of the publication, using the creative experience as part of the narrative. The on-site spontaneity is a good hook, giving a somewhat bland story a bit of character, as well as providing a built-in photo layout opportunity.

Former booker for the "Joan Rivers Show," "Today," and presently with "A Closer Look," Stuart Krasnow is attracted to pitches that have energy and excitement. "It's not just 'Come cover the dog show' or 'Come and see how dog food is made.' It's 'Hi, we have a computer that matches animals and owners and we can take three guests and have them fill out these surveys, and then bring out three dogs, and then the computer matches the dogs to the guests.' Now that can be fun."

When you sit down to write your pitch, being creative doesn't stop with one idea. In pitching, there is more than one way to shape your story option. Story options are your insurance policies. They buy you more discussion time, increase your chances of getting placement, and prove to the media that the guest is not just one-dimensional, which allows the media to feel confident that the story won't fall on its face. And, if he can't accommodate your idea at that time, an editor or producer is more likely to put your pitch with the various options in the "save file" because it gives him something for down the line. You never know what is going on in the heads of editors or producers. If you are pitching something five different ways, four ways might not apply to the paper's editorial schedule or the show's format, but the fifth one may fit nicely into a story concept they may already be developing.

THEMES, TRENDS, ROUNDUPS, AND UMBRELLA STORIES ARE OPTIONS

Themes, trends, roundups, and umbrella stories are all basically the same thing. These inclusive categories suggest that, along with your client or product, there are others in the same field to round out your story idea. This is a great way to pitch the media should your client or product not be able to stand alone in a story.

If you are planning the story idea and you cannot come up with any other client or products to include, don't panic. Just suggest the idea. The producer or editor may have other similar requests on file or may be looking for another idea for an already planned roundup.

There are pros and cons to being grouped if you don't already have visibility. As for the pros, this is a way to begin building your media kit reprints. Also, the group in which you'll be included may give you a new level of respect in the marketplace. And, as I said before, being grouped may be the only way to begin getting coverage. But the con is that there is no guarantee that just because you pitched the story, your client will be well-positioned in the story. Remember what your goals are and try to evaluate what role a client will play in a group before you pitch the idea. Beware of the cons.

PITCH LETTER ETIQUETTE

- Tailor the pitch letter! Erik Himmelsbach, editor, *Orange Coast Magazine*, is convinced that people have one pitch letter they use for every media. "It's better if it's all personalized. You give more attention to a personalized letter than to a form letter. If it's a typed envelope and a typed letter, you will get more attention than if a label that has been spit out by a computer was used. If it says, 'Hey, Eric Himmelsbach, this is what's happening and this is why your magazine would be great for my client and vice versa,' it gives me more of a reason to pay attention to it."

- Don't send out letters addressed "Dear Colleague" or "Dear Associate" or any other generic term.

- Don't have the "Dear Mr." or "Mrs." or "Ms." offset or copied along with the rest of the letter and then hand-type the appropriate name in the blank space, especially if the typeface doesn't even match!

- Be sure that your salutation and text is appropriate to the media you're sending it to. Don't make the mistake of sending a pitch starting with "Dear Editors" to radio or TV people. Follow through appropriately in the body of your letter. Don't request an on-air interview if the addressee is print media.

A pitch letter is just that—a letter. Don't make it a segment script, a feature article, or an authorized biography on your client's life. It is a carefully choreographed, written conversation to pique the interest, to whet the appetite of the media enough so that they will want to interview the subject.

It is a sales tool in the form of an invitation, a tease to make the media want to get the story.

THE PITCH LETTER FORMAT

A pitch letter follows the form of a formal business letter. It should be informative (covering the basic who, what, where, when, and why), concise and to the point, no more than two hundred words (12 to 15 lines), and carefully divided into three or four paragraphs. It has a salutation, a sign-off, and a signature.

Note: The optimum pitch letter is one hundred words.

THE FIRST PARAGRAPH The first paragraph identifies the topic for discussion. It can also contain the request for coverage, in which case there is no need to repeat it again in the body.

The first paragraph is the most important. *Avoid schmoozing* in the first paragraph—it wastes valuable time. Most of the media people I interviewed said they would throw away the letter if the opening paragraph didn't get to the point. They hate looking for what the pitch is about. Normally the media decide within seconds if it gets into the yes, no, or maybe pile. They get an overwhelming amount of mail and they have to cut through it very quickly. Many times I was told, "One knows immediately what will work and what won't."

THE MIDDLE PARAGRAPH The middle paragraph(s) explains the reason you are sending the letter, what your story option(s) is(are). The body of the pitch letter is there to sell the subject. Zig Ziglar, sales instructor extraordinaire, tells us that the best salesperson knows people well enough to know what they need and what motivates them and how to provide it. The body of the letter is where you accomplish this. Remember, you should also be sending along a media kit, so make the body of the pitch letter light on background information.

THE LAST PARAGRAPH The last paragraph wraps up the dialogue and sets the tone for what is being requested. This paragraph is not needed if you have already stated your purpose in the first or lead-in paragraph.

THE SIGN-OFF   The sign-off informs the reader how you intend to proceed with the business of follow-up. It is posturing, it is intent, and you must be careful and diplomatic when you write your sign-off. If you write "I know that you will be fascinated with the project," although you are trying to show an optimistic attitude, it may be construed as your making the decision for them before they have a chance to think about it—that you are manipulating them. Here are some all-time favorite sign-offs from the professionals:

"I LOOK FORWARD TO CONTINUING THIS CONVERSATION [OR DIALOGUE]."
—RALEIGH PINSKEY
"I LOOK FORWARD TO HEARING FROM YOU AT YOUR EARLIEST CONVENIENCE."
—JOANNE SMALE
"I'VE INCLUDED SOME REPRINTS FOR YOUR PERUSAL AND I'LL GIVE YOU A CALL SHORTLY FOR YOUR THOUGHTS."
—JESSICA JOSELL
"I WILL TAKE THE LIBERTY OF FOLLOWING UP THIS CORRESPONDENCE WITH A TELEPHONE CALL TO DISCUSS THE POSSIBILITIES."
—JOSHUA SIMONS

How About Using Colored Paper for Releases and Pitch Letters?

Publicist Flo Selfman has a confession to make. She wasn't a colored paper sender when she first started, but she has become one, favoring bright pink, blue, and yellow for impact. She even consults with her clients on their color choice. In response to the typical media statement, "We get so much mail," she feels that when you call to follow up, you can say, "It's on bright pink paper," and they can reach into that huge pile and put their hand on it in a second. That's the reason why many PR people send colored paper. Not only does she feel it makes a difference on arrival, she also knows that it makes following up much easier. No one can ignore a bright pink release. And besides, she has fun.

Now, on the other hand, Brian Lewis, editor of the *Los Angeles Independent*, says that colored paper doesn't matter to him. Yes, it may help him find it faster in a pile when he gets calls for follow-up, but it doesn't make an impression when he is deciding to print it or not to print it.

Note: Colored paper is harder to recycle.

Faxing Releases and Pitch Letters

With postage costs rising and voice mail making it more difficult to talk to the real thing, faxes have definitely catapulted the art of doing business into a new dimension. It is true that publicists are now engaged in "faxmania." Not only are they sending releases, they are sending entire media kits with reprints, bios, and minifeatures. This is the age of *instant gratification*, a publicist's dream…but media's nightmare! More and more media are not giving out their fax numbers unless they ask for the materials. Private machines with private numbers are now replacing the general machines, with materials sent on the general number sitting for hours or days until someone checks it. What could have been a gentle giant is slowly turning into a closed door faster than we can say, "Fax it!" As a media friend told me, "Yes, I get faxes, boy do I get faxes. I get a fax telling me they are sending the fax. Then I get a call asking if I got the fax. It would be OK if I asked for the fax in the first place, but these aren't faxes I asked for, let alone want to get. Junk faxes, I'm getting junk faxes, things that are pertinent to nothing and could have come in the mail. It's like the flack who cried wolf." The media asked me to champion their frustrated cry: "WE STILL GET DAILY MAIL DELIVERY." A word to the wise: Keep a record of who likes releases faxed and who doesn't.

9

Using Gimmicks to Assist Your Pitch

"I enjoyed playing with the battery-operated hand that crawled across my desk while the middle finger beckoned me to come closer. But the movie was still a terrible movie and there was nothing I could do for it."
—Bob Levitan, producer, "It's Fritz"

Gorillas delivering gingersnaps, Prince Charming handing out pizza, crawling hands holding caramels—these are the types of hooks that the PR and media refer to as gimmicks. Gimmicks also include key chains, mirrors, lighters, etc., printed or embossed with the name of your client, his product, etc. Generally the media look at gimmicks as an attempt to cover up the fact that there is not much else to sell. If what you are selling is inherently good, then you shouldn't need the gimmick. Some feel that a gimmick doesn't necessarily hurt, and in some cases it might get something to stand out, but that doesn't mean the media will cover your client simply because they liked the gimmick. The value of gimmicks is sort of like the value of colored paper for releases.

If you are going to go to the expense of using a gimmick, come up with something that people will be able to use or will keep on their desk within view. The media recognize that the point is to keep the client's name visible, but the gimmick should not be ostentatious nor should the name be too visible. Gold-plated picture frames and clocks with company names on them are considered inappropriate and a waste. "If it didn't have the name of the company on it I would have taken it home and used it," was the common comment.

WHY SEND GIMMICKS?   The only two reasons I could dig out of the media that had any positive value were that gimmicks would be something to get the word out on the project and perhaps would act as a PR goodwill gesture.

WHY NOT SEND GIMMICKS?   Hardly anyone remembered which campaign it was for if it wasn't written on the gimmick, and many gave away the gimmick if it had the campaign written on it. If it doesn't get the kind of reaction that supports your aim or your goal it is a waste.

Gimmicks are conversation starters, but if it's a bad gimmick it can boomerang, much like flattery. All you want to do is get the media's attention. After that the project or client is going to stand or fall on how appropriate it is for the media. Even if sending the gimmicks doesn't hurt, they usually don't help as much as you might think they do.

Note: Be aware that what you send is a gift, and a gift only, and you know what they say about gifts? Once you give it, it belongs to the person you gave it to, and they can do whatever they want with it, including giving it away, throwing it away, and not considering it a reason to cover your client. My advice is that there are better ways to spend money. Spend it on advertising, or spend it on a good photographer!

A TV producer who asked to remain nameless has a combined family totaling eighteen people. Every year he puts together a huge grab bag of all the gimmicks he got over the year and distributes them among the family at Christmas Eve dinner. Another producer saves them and donates them to needy children. And still another sells them at a garage sale he holds once a year.

On the Sending of Gorillas, Belly Dancers, and Bunnywabbits

OK. The campaign is brilliant, the media kit is definitely pizzazzy, the photos are captivating and expressive, the pitch letter is right on target...and then you stuff all of these sizzling elements into a No. Five Jiffy Bag that makes it look like all the rest of the packages the media gets on its holding desk.

Life is unfair, you say? So you contemplate stickering the outside with gorillas or balloons, just to have an edge, in hopes of evoking a positive response before they open your package. And then the thought strikes you, why *sticker* with a gorilla or balloons—why not the real thing? And you remember the back of your local magazine with all the advertisements for the wonderful balloons and gorillas and belly dancers.

Well, before you go any further, read this, because you might decide to go and work out your creative frustration at a make-your-own ice-cream sundae bar.

If delivery gimmicks are looked on only as a showcase for the publicist's creativity, and the only thing they seem to create in the eyes of the media is disdain toward the one who sent them, then gorillas, belly dancers, and balloons seem to be definite no-no's.

"Live With Regis and Kathie Lee" producer Michael Gelman isn't impressed by delivery stunts. Yes, he agrees they command more attention than a simple media release would, but he doesn't think they're worth the effort, the expense, or the annoyance they can create in an office.

Marianne Goldstein of the *New York Post* told of how the book companies would send Santa to give out books at Christmas. "It was cute," she agreed, "but it didn't make me more likely to mention the book in my column." Once upon a

time there was a book about Prince Charming so the publisher's publicist sent someone dressed as Prince Charming to
kiss all the girls. "Sure, you groan, but it did make me smile.
But I didn't write about the book."

Brian Lewis, editor of the *Los Angeles Independent*, thinks
gimmicks are amusing, but questionable in terms of ethics. A
reporter shouldn't be influenced by accepting any sort of gifts
or payola.

But it is *USA Today*'s Tom Green who says it all on the
subject of balloons, gorillas, and belly dancers: "We really
don't want those...I mean we really don't want those!"

10

The Art of Follow-Up

"The clothes won't get in the drawer unless you put them there."
—My mother

Why Do Follow-Up?

Follow-up means just that—you call to insure that the ball will continue rolling once you set it in motion. Follow-up is making sure that the media does the thing you made them get off their duff to do.

Wouldn't it be wonderful if you could just put the media kit components in a preglued envelope, stick on a mailing label, stamp it, send it on its way, and then just sit back and wait for the clipping service to send you mounds and mounds of print and video clips? I'd sure go for that. Features, reviews, best bets, profiles, gossip bits, trend stories, roundups, field pieces, in-studio performances, and whatever else, just pouring out of an overflowing mail bag? A publicist's dream!

If you don't call and engage the media in meaningful dialogue (unless they are so interested that they call you immediately upon getting your release), the chances of your getting covered are very slim indeed.

Following up gives you that opportunity to alter the proposal to their immediate needs. It also shows them you care about what you are working on.

It plants the seeds for a continuing relationship.

It will teach you more about the person on your mailing list than you can learn in any other way.

Follow-Up comes in two flavors:

1. Checking to see if whatever you sent has arrived.
2. Engaging the media in a dialogue to motivate them to consider your pitch if they haven't already made their decision, or helping them to alter their decision if it is not in your favor.

These are not necessarily two separate calls. If the person you need to speak with is there, by all means talk to them right then and there. In fact, one should always be prepared that either they will answer their own phone or the receptionist will automatically switch you to them.

WHY FOLLOW UP TO SEE IF IT GOT THERE?

This is the twentieth century, and one would assume that if you have gotten your return receipt requested from the post office, the fax transaction record from your machine, the signature from UPS or Federal Express, and the code number from the messenger service, that you can rest assured that what you sent not only arrived, but was forwarded to the proper person named on the envelope. Don't be too naive.

Check, not only to cover yourself, but also for these reasons that I have heard and collected on my follow-up journeys:

• Gee, I don't seem to have it. When did you send it?
• I wonder if it may have gotten buried under another pile on someone's desk?
• Maybe I accidentally filed it incorrectly. What was the name again?
• Yeah, I was on vacation and I can't seem to locate half my stuff, and besides, now I've gotten backed up and I don't have time to look for it, can you send me another one?

- Oh, yes, I remember wanting to open that one to-day...now where did I put it?
- I signed for it? Well, whadda ya know!

Sad but true. So I go by the premise that all media are conscientious but overworked. Not everyone has the luxury of a secretary or an intern.

Be careful on how you handle giving the name of the person who signed for the package, should you need to. The call to verify may be looked upon as bad enough, but if you have to give a name, it has the potential as coming off as a confrontation. It's like saying, "I know you got it, don't lie to me, why don't you admit it?" And you don't want to be perceived this way, ever.

Following up to see if the package got there can, however, be a feather in your cap, in that it shows the person on the other side that this endeavor has your total support. You have not just thrown it against the wall—it deserves their attention, and one way or another they are going to have to deal with it. Even though they may not want to be bothered, they do respect someone who is conscientious and professional.

WHEN LEAVING A MESSAGE ON DATED MATERIAL

The likelihood of someone opening your material upon arrival is slim. Not impossible, but slim. As a general rule, expect opening to take anywhere from a day to a week. If someone is coming to town to promote their product very soon, you want to convey this by *boldly* marking DATED MATERIAL on the outside. The media are usually good about opening such packages immediately. However, never forget that we are always in the Murphy's Law mode, and it is usually your package that slips through the crack. So...call immediately, if not sooner.

The department receptionist may be assigned to the log-in position. If you feel that the person you speak with doesn't have a handle on the situation because you hear words such as "maybe" or "I guess," *politely* suggest that you speak with someone who works directly with the person to whom the material was sent. I cannot stress strongly enough the use of the word *suggest* instead of *demand*, because even as you speak to them this person could be promoted to that very next position. Trust me, they will remember you and your telephone demeanor.

On Deadlines

One of the meanest voices you will ever encounter is if you call the media and they are on deadline. There is a grunt, a primal scream of the "I'm on deadline" followed by the loudest click you ever heard.

Finding out when deadline happens is no mystery. You merely ask the receptionist. Sounds simple, but before you go dialing the receptionist you must realize that there are several kinds of deadlines:

- individual writer deadlines
- column deadlines
- feature deadlines
- closing deadlines
- research deadlines
- photo deadlines
- "I'm leaving in five minutes" deadlines
- various incidental deadlines that are difficult to pinpoint

When calling to find out the deadline, *be sure you ask for editorial deadlines, not advertising*.

THE THREE WORST TIMES TO CALL (OTHER THAN DEADLINES)

- The "early morning don't call me because I'm working in quiet" time.

- The "I'm trying to eat my lunch in peace" time.
- The "why do they always call me on Fridays? Don't they know I'm cleaning off my desk from the week and planning next week?" time.

SOLVING THE DEADLINE PROBLEM

1. Ask: What is your personal deadline?
   What is your section deadline?
   Which is your busiest day?
   What is your busiest time of day?
   What time don't you want me to call you?
   What time do you leave?
   Do you take calls during lunch?
   Do you take calls early in the morning?
   What day is your staff pitching meeting?
   What time does your meeting begin and end?
   When is the optimum time to call?

Note: Do realize, however, that each day is completely different from the next, even when that day has been specified as the ultimate day and time to call. Remember that we all have free will, and the right to use it. And they will.

2. Make file cards on the above questions and answers

I learned this trick when I did radio promotion for a record label. In order to remember each of the four hundred stations' pitching days, listening days, pitching times, and playlist deadline days, I kept a three-by-five-inch card on everyone. The card also served for birthdays and personality hints. Now I maintain a similar file on every media, editor, booker, and producer I work with, only now I do it on a computer.

If You Think Follow-Up Is a Chance to Chat—Don't

If you think that a follow-up call means it's time to schmooze and make nice, flatter and cajole, you have another thing coming. By now you know that even if you know the person on the other end, they are probably busy. Unless you are calling to confirm plans to meet for lunch, forget it. As B. L. Ochman put it: "Schmoozing is fine, for four seconds. Cut to the chase."

Follow-up calls are business calls and should be considered extensions of the pitch letter. This doesn't mean you can't be humorous or friendly, but learn to convey that in your greeting, and whatever the next phrase you use to personalize your conversation before you move to the point at hand. Otherwise you could take up so much time schmoozing that there is no time for the pitch and you could lose your golden opportunity.

Furthermore, media people hate you to assume that you are bosom buddies and have been for a lifetime. It ranks right up there with misspelling their name, calling at deadline, and not knowing the needs of their particular media.

The Follow-Up Voice

When the publicist goes into what is unaffectionately known as the "follow-up voice" mode, the media goes out of listening mode.

A "follow-up voice" can be characterized by impersonal, efficient, and calculated vocalizations, as if something is being read as opposed to being discussed. The pitch voice seems to have a mind of its own. I find that it tries to take over my carefully manicured professional voice, especially when I am talking with someone I don't know or haven't dealt with before.

A "follow-up voice" is characterized by a singsongy, driven rhythm that sounds phony and rehearsed. Think back to the call that interrupts you at dinner, the one where they want to sell you something you don't need, want, or desire. You recognize the voice immediately and want to hang up. That's a "follow-up voice."

Another "follow-up voice" is characterized by whining. Don't whine—it comes across as manipulative. Of course, your version of whining and theirs could be different, depending on if they had a good time last night, or whether they liked what they had for lunch. But it does exist in their minds, and that is all that counts. It's all a gamble at a certain level, but try to stack the odds in your favor.

How to Make Your Follow-Up Voice Meaningful

The media may be many things, but they are not stupid. They know that the client is selling something—that we want something from them. So what does it take to personalize your voice, just like you did in the pitch? Make them feel that it is right for them and not just that you need to get your client as much exposure as possible, even though that is what you are doing. They know we have a job to do; we're not fooling them, so don't try. It's the game of courtship in a different arena, that's all.

Try to sound happy to be there. Who knows, maybe it will carry over. The fact that you sound like you have given a little time, thought, and effort to why your client would be right for them over and above anyone else obviously makes them feel as if they have something special being offered to them. It might get you an extra minute's consideration. If nothing else, it paves the path for the next time you call.

How do you avoid that insincere, canned, singsongy sound? How do you make it sound meaningful? Easy. You did it in your pitch letter, didn't you? Practice into a tape recorder— you may be amazed by what you sound like. Tape yourself on the phone and listen with a critical ear. The insincerity I am referring to will become immediately apparent.

Preparing for the Phone Call

Getting ready to make a follow-up call is a similar exercise to packing a suitcase. First you assemble the necessary items for survival, and then you add in the luxury items. After you have laid them out, the rule of thumb is to remove one half of everything, wait a day, and make one more cut, usually one third of what is left.

In this spirit:

1. Take out your pitch letter and highlight the points you want to get across. This means only the key phrases, the basics, the who, what, where, when, and why.

2. Go over it again to determine if there is another salient point or catch phrase you would like to include.

3. Go over it again to see if there is something else you can delete.

Knowing What You Should Know Before You Call

- Know your business, but more than that, know their business.
- Know the subject inside and out, backward and forward.
- Know the kind of people you are dealing with, both the client and the person to whom you are pitching.
- Have enough confidence and enthusiasm about your client without going overboard and turning the media off.
- Know that people are apprehensive to make a decision when it doesn't fall into a given structure. You have to do their thinking for them. Show them how you can do it for them.
- Know what their language is—be receptive to their buzz words—and put it into your discussion in the context of what you are trying to present. Use succinct terms that they understand.
- Learn the parameters so that when you have two minutes to nail somebody down you know how to play by the rules.
- Know that timing is of the essence.

Note: Remember that what you are doing is selling, and the final part of the sale is making sure they know that if they decide to do something with you, you can deliver. Be in a position to help them out and hold their hands until it is over and put to bed.

And Now, It's That Time!

So, you have gotten all your lists together, your pencils are sharpened, you have a red pen for corrections and notes, and you have removed all liquids from your desk so you won't accidentally spill anything on your lists.

You have reviewed the section on knowing the media and you feel confident that you have done your homework about who you are going to talk to, what they do, and how they do it.

You have studied your pitch letter, highlighted it, and put it in front of you at a comfortable angle.

You have practiced the pitch into a tape recorder so you know how you sound.

You have asked the receptionist to hold your calls or you have put your other line on machine pickup.

You have gone to the bathroom.

You know deep down in your heart that this is important to you, and right for the person you are calling.

When to Use the "A" Motivation Speech

Know that you can't approach everything with the same level of intensity. There are some things which get the "A pitch." And you can't tell this to your client, but you have to know when to push. Someone who calls the media with every little idea hampers his or her reputation.

A prominent national editor likes it when people are selective with what they call her about. "The best PR people call twice a year. They have a track record with you of having a good story, they don't call unnecessarily, and you know that if they do call it is going to be important. They tell you right away who they are, what they are calling about, what they want—and if it's a person on tour, when they will be in town." Gannett's Kerry Schaffer doesn't want to be called unless it is really a story. "Don't even try and call, and don't pull an 'I don't think you would be interested, but...' call. We probably won't. Don't try me." Paulette Weiss of *Where Magazine* says, "If you're going to be a 'calling pest,' you run the risk of losing your credibility for the next time. So if you are going to call, think this thing out very carefully. Think if it is a good call for the particular media you are calling. Don't just throw your ball in the wind. Really, don't call unless there is some chance of it really winding up being done."

Making Contact

Picture yourself in a lounge chair by the pool, sipping a mint julep with the person who is about to get on the phone. When you get connected:

1. identify yourself and your client.
2. ask if they have a few seconds to discuss it.
3. give it to them straight.

They really appreciate it when you ask them if they have a few seconds or if they are on the other line. It proves your awareness. Chances are, if they are on another call and you have been considerate, they will put you on hold, finish the other conversation, and come back to you. That one little sentence after your qualifying salutation can throw a whole different light on your business relationship.

As Gannett's Barbara Nachman tells it, she hates when people act as if she is a tape recorder. She hates when they call up and spew out the whole thing, not waiting to hear if she's on the other line or on deadline. As she categorizes the contact attempt, "It's akin to verbal diarrhea." To make sure you don't put yourself in that position, ask a question like:

- Do you have a second?
- I hope I didn't catch you at a bad time?
- I truly only need a second of your time.
- Can we talk now, or are you on the other line?
- I hope I'm not interrupting anything.
- Are you on deadline?

These must not be said in supplication. No begging sounds allowed. These queries are to be put forth as a plain and simple courtesy.

Note: Qualify the purpose of your call *before* you ask if they have a few seconds to listen.

Radio and television programs only have four to eight seconds to catch the listener's attention before they switch to another station. Media have a time frame or window after which they, too, switch off from listening to you. It is best if you can deliver your basic contact information in less than fifteen seconds. This allows you approximately fifty words, the bare bones for you to let them know the who, what, where, when, and why of your call. Remember, you have them on the phone, now.

> "I SENT MATERIALS ON JAZZ GREAT JACKIE MCLEAN—HE'S IN TOWN TO PLAY THE CLASSIC JAZZ SERIES AT LINCOLN CENTER ON AUGUST 4TH AND I WOULD LIKE HIM ON YOUR SHOW ANYTIME THE WEEK BEFORE." (9 SECONDS)

> "I SENT MATERIALS ON THE T. J. MARTELL CELEBRITY BOWLING PARTY ON MAY 5TH, AND I'M HOPING YOU WILL COME AND COVER IT." (6 SECONDS)

> "I REPRESENT SAM'S AUX LAIT, AND I SENT YOU A MEDIA KIT FOR YOUR ARTICLE ON COFFEE BARS. HAVE YOU HAD A CHANCE TO LOOK AT IT YET? (7 SECONDS)

As for them not receiving your materials:

- Suggest sending them another package immediately. If they hem and haw, take the bull by the horns, tell them it's no problem, and either messenger it or overnight it. If they offer their billing number, it's OK to take it.
- Ask if you may fax the pitch and one or two pages of background.
- Check the address and get the fax number.
- Ask how long after they receive it can you call again.
- Sign off with a thank you for their time.

Note: If you discover that you forgot to get their fax number or address, *get it from the receptionist—don't bother them again.*

Alternative Ways to Ask If They Are Going to Run It

Jane Gilman of the *Larchmont Chronicle* doesn't blame people for trying, but she doesn't appreciate them calling and asking, "Did you get that release and are you going to run it?" She feels that it puts her on the defensive, which is a ridiculous position to find oneself when answering the phone. "They can ask if I got the release," she tells me, "but asking me if I'm going to run it is in very poor taste and very unprofessional."

I took a poll and put together suggestions from both sides as to how to ask the question in more professional terms. Here are some suggestions:

So, what did you think of my idea?

Are you interested in the piece?

Is it something you think can fit into your format?

Are you open to discussing it further?

Is this an open or closed dialogue?

How to Gauge the Contact

How do you know if they are happy or sad? How can you tell if they have just spilled coffee on themselves and all over their desk? How do you know if they are late for a meeting or in a meeting or wished they were in a meeting? I can only tell you to hear rhythm in their voices. Feel what they are feeling without telling them what they are feeling. Hear that they are rushed, that they are tired, that they have another phone call and even that they are hating talking to you at that moment. Be secure and in the moment. Give them space. Tell them you will call back when they have more time, even though this is your moment. And don't hold it over their heads. Don't even mention it when you call the next time.

Gannett's Barbara Nachman cautions you to listen to the give and take of the pitch conversation, not just to your side. She was pitched with an idea which she quickly realized was a story, but as a reporter she needed to pass it by her editor. She told the woman that she thought it was a story, but that she just needed confirmation from her editor. The woman would not stop. She kept going on and on with more facts and more angles. Nachman raised her voice and told her again that she thought it was a good idea, but still the woman wouldn't stop and continued to sell something that was already sold. "If I wasn't a professional," Ms. Nachman told me, "I would have rescinded my offer."

Persistence

Media respect persistence in getting them on the phone, but they have no respect for those who persist after the project has been discussed, reworked, and rejected. Don't send client updates unless the news is genuinely important; don't have another colleague speak out on your behalf; don't send personal notes, gifts, or theater tickets. An overly persistent attitude is self-defeating, both for you and your client.

The Philosophy of Rejection

"Every show gets countless submissions from people who think that what they have done is the most important thing in the world," was a typical comment in my interviews with the media. Les Sinclair, producer of the "Merv Griffin Show," explained that "producers find it is much easier to say no because it is the producer who is on the line if the client turns out to be a turkey. Producers tend to play it safe."

The worst thing that someone can do when facing a refusal is to exhibit great discomfort or dissatisfaction. This is universally considered an attempt at a guilt trip, and that can only be detrimental to your future. As Lyle Gregory, producer for "The Michael Jackson Show," told me, "A stressed out, disappointed rejectee is not welcome here. Neither is it going to change my answer."

Michael Gelman wants you to know that you should not take any rejection personally, unless so specified. His advice, "You can't take it personally, you just have to move on. Think of it as a numbers game. Just don't whine!"

Humor is appreciated, if you are not being facetious. But be careful, it's a fine line. But when it works, it eases the tension, making it a win-win situation. Los Angeles publicist Julie Nathanson never takes a refusal personally, instead she tries to infuse the situation with humor. She has been known to tell the media "you'll hear from me in March of 1997."

My usual is, "Moooving right along!" Depending on who it is I might say, "This is your last chance…" I've even told them, "Now don't hold back, tell me how you really feel!" No matter how things turn out I always offer a thank you, and tell them I'll be in touch.

Voice Mail and Machine Etiquette

Lyle Gregory of "The Michael Jackson Show" would prefer that you don't leave six-minute messages on his voice mail. He also wishes that everyone who left a message would always write it out before they call and bring it down to between twenty and thirty seconds. His guidelines:

- Keep your voice up, crisp, quick, and to the point.
- Speak slowly when you give the phone number.
- Give name and number first, message next and end with name and number, so the recipient doesn't have to rewind to hear the number again in order to write it down. When leaving the name and number, be clear and concise, don't mumble, and don't hurry through as if they know it already. You may know it, they don't.

Many of the media stressed that you should always leave some indication about the subject of your call. If you thought they wouldn't return your call if they knew what the topic was, they certainly weren't going to return your call if you didn't leave an indication. It especially irritates them if they call back and find that it is some topic they are not in the mood to deal with. At least if they know what it is about, they can act accordingly, which prompts a win-win situation.

I was amazed to find that the topic "how to leave a phone message" interested so many people in the media. It seems to be an art form all its own, and a forgotten one at that, with not many people knowing how to participate on a competent level.

A phone message should contain the basic who, what, where, when, and why:

- Hello, my name is Raleigh Pinskey
- I am calling from The Raleigh Group, Ltd., in Los Angeles
- My telephone number is (213) 555-7144
- This message is for Clay Smith
- I'm calling about the media kit I sent on Jackie McLean. He will be in Los Angeles at Catalina's July 17th to the 22nd, and I would like "Entertainment Tonight" to come to Catalina's and do a story on him.

- Again, my name is Raleigh Pinskey. R-A-L-E-I-G-H P-I-N-S-K-E-Y.
- From The Raleigh Group, Ltd.
- My phone number in Los Angeles is (213) 555-7144.

And If They Don't Return Your Calls?

Rude as it seems, many media do not return your calls if they are not interested in what you have to offer them. And they definitely won't return your call if you don't indicate the subject in your message. Sometimes you just have to leave it alone after your initial call, if you know this to be their modus operandi. If you are not familiar with the media, I'd give them no more than two calls, three if your ego is involved. Try checking with the secretary or receptionist as to how the person works.

Depending on what the project is and how strongly I feel it rightfully belongs with that particular media, I will send another package with a handwritten note saying, "Perhaps you didn't receive the first package. I feel there is audience payoff from this project. Hope you find it interesting. I'll check back with you." But I caution you that you can easily irritate them with this. Those media that don't believe in the courtesy of a return call can perceive you as being too aggressive, despite the fact that the media tells you they want you to be aggressive when it comes to following up.

Cold-Calling: What It Is and When to Use It

Many in the media are known to be so busy that they do not open their mail, waiting instead for you to make your follow-up calls, at which time they claim that the media kit has not yet crossed their desk. Or, they do open their mail, but because they are not interested in the project at that moment it gets tossed in the circular file, and because they get an average of thirty media kits a day, they don't remember that they have seen it.

I have learned to print twenty percent more media kits than the mailing list dictates because of the "media throw away factor." Materials, postage, messengers, phone calls, and time are a huge cost factor for the client, and stuffing, sealing, labeling, and calling is a big time factor for the publicist. Many publicists consider the "media throw away factor" as cold war tactics and have devised a means by which to combat it. It is called cold-calling.

Cold-calling is when you deliberately have not sent your media kit, and yet you call to follow-up on your "mailing." Patty Neger of "Good Morning America" would like to have materials before she is called. She knows that publicists have taken to calling before sending because of the remail nuisance factor, but she reads everything she sets and if you tell her you have sent the information, it makes her feel as if she is losing her sanity if she can't identify your release.

The *New York Times*'s Angela Dodson advises everyone that it will do them no good to get through to her directly with an oral presentation. She can't concentrate on its value, which interferes with the possibility that she will act on it. A release on paper has a stronger impact. Dodson isn't the only one who won't assign space for something someone has discussed on the phone. And yet there are many media who are open to this method of follow-up.

The following dialogue actually occurred between a prominent publicist and a prominent media person.

P: Let's say that someone calls for a follow-up on a media release and they say, "Hello, did you get the release I sent you on such and such?"

M: And I lie and I say, "Yes, I did, and I'm keeping it on file and I don't know what I'm doing with it." "I'm sorry," she says to me, "but it does save me a lot of trouble."

P: Well, let me tell you what I do. I have learned that there are all kinds of people at the other end of the phone and it is very difficult to judge what is real and what is not to every single person. And I have learned to call up people and say, "Hi, I've sent you press materials on blah blah and I would like to discuss the possibility of us doing something together." But, of course, in reality I have never sent it.

M: And then I say, "Yes, I got it and I'm keeping it on file." And then you know who's a liar? Oh, dear me, I've been caught.

P: And then you'll say, "Gee, I don't recognize the subject matter, when did you send it?" And I'll say, "Last week, that's enough time for you to have gotten it, isn't it?" And then you would say, "Not for this office, and I don't see it. Would you be kind enough to send me another one?" And I say, "Of course, I would." I send it out immediately with *re-sent per your request* on the outside and a brief personal Post-it note on the inside.

Note: Cold-calling for "follow-up" is a cheater's way of doing things. Because mail and faxes can get lost or misrouted, there is an element of reality in this method. Be careful, however. Choose your moment, choose your media, and don't falter.

11

Interviews

"When the reporter puts down the microphone, closes the notepad, and puts the pen in the pocket, it may be that the interview is just beginning."
—Jack Popejoy, KFWB Radio, Los Angeles

A reporter shared with me an amusing and revealing theory about interviews. The theory is that there are at least six people present in a conventional two-party conversation: the two principals and both their sets of parents (the spirit of the parents' influence, that is). A media interview, then, may very well expand that theoretical number to nine if we add the editor, the publisher, and the publicist. Funny as this may sound, all of these people do have a stake in the interview, so, in a sense, they are all present.

Interviews are the pot of gold at the end of the rainbow. Interviews are your payoff. Doesn't it make sense, then, to try and collect all that you are entitled to get? The formula for giving a good interview is no secret. It can be summed up in one word: preparation. Because there are numerous comprehensive books dealing with media appearances and the interview process, I would just like to emphasize several areas that I feel are crucial to getting the most out of an interview.

How to Prepare for a Radio or TV Interview

On several print media opportunities and radio talk shows I was able to expand my client's coverage by columns, pages, and minutes when I had researched the interviewer's agenda and preferences. My client and I could then use this knowledge as a tool, shaping our information to be more "interviewer friendly."

Knowing how the interviewer and the media thinks is your best defense. Read three or more issues of the magazine or newspaper, or watch an entire show. Study three or more pieces the particular interviewer has written for the magazine, newspaper, or TV show. This should give you an overview of the specifics of the media's agenda as well as what interview methods they employ. Ask yourself the following questions:

- Do they allow the guest to finish her train of thought or do they cut off the speaker?
- Do they use the element of surprise to flip into private questions, or do they attempt to disarm with the sincere approach?
- Do they try to complete their agenda by returning to the questions they want answered, even though the guest has said he or she won't answer them?
- If there is no on-air personality, do they weave soundbites, taking them out of context, shaping an interview into something entirely different from the one the guest thought he had given?
- Does the interviewer appear to know the subject? Does he allow the subject to lead the interview, stepping in only to comment on what is said, or does he begin by provoking the guest into what the interviewer wants answered?

And If You Don't Like the Interviewer?

If I find the interviewer suitable and appropriate for my client, I will approve the interview. If not, I will ask for another interviewer. If I can't get another, I will strongly advise the client against doing the interview. If the media wouldn't give me another choice, and the one they assigned was not suitable, in my judgment, I would definitely cancel the piece. A bad interview, like a bad review, can be damaging to a career. Better no story than a story that harms you or your client.

Unfortunately, recommending your own choice for the interviewer leaves some editors speculating that you feel their judgment is not good, and, of course, this perception is true. After all, if every media person was all sweetness and kindness they would be called puffs and not critics. Suggesting your own choice of interviewer is a tricky business. Even if you propose a list of three, four, or five from which the editor could choose, they are still your choices and not the editor's. If you can substantiate your reasons for not wanting the one he selected, an editor may honor that decision but still not go with the one you selected. A good editor will ask why the publicist does not want a specific writer. Taking the reasons into account and then making the decision with both sides in mind is a very good example of a collaboration, although Jonathan Alter of *Newsweek* feels that it is a sell-out when an editor allows a publicist to have a say in who writes the story. At that point, he feels that the editor might just as well be letting the publicist edit the publication and the editor has no right to call himself an editor. He acknowledges that it is the publicist's right to try and write the story by choosing who she wants, but he definitely feels it is the editor's right not to comply.

Can You Control the Content of the Questions?

Watch how quickly the media decides how badly they want to do an interview, when the client or publicist starts making content demands. If the interview is with someone who will boost ratings but doesn't want to talk about her private life, this will most likely be OK because the show wants to interview her anyway. But, if it is not a VIP interviewee and she starts calling the shots, then the media may decide not to interview her. I believe that the publicist or the client has to have some rights when it comes to content, so ask politely. Be aware that the media may agree to bypass the issue but then stick it to you during the show.

Ask yourself this question: What purpose am I trying to achieve by doing this interview? The answer to this question will help you define your agenda, allowing you to discern whether it suits your purpose to answer certain questions or discuss certain topics.

Never forget that a reporter is there to do a job, and that job only gets done by asking questions. Because reporters report what you tell them in a manner that will satisfy their objectives and the objectives of their media, your responsibility as the one who is being interviewed is to say only those things that will further your agenda, to help you achieve your objectives equally as well as the media's. There is no need to be afraid to say that you don't want to answer any question. You are not there to please the interviewer. But if you won't or can't comment, just say so—never hedge. Jack Popejoy, reporter for KFWB radio, Los Angeles, put together these suggestions for how *not* to answer a question. Say:

- I refuse. [If you are really going to refuse.]
- I'm sorry, but I can't answer that question. It is a proprietary matter and I am not in a position to respond to that publicly.
- It is a personal matter.
- That matter is under litigation and I can't answer that question now.

- I'm not the best person to answer that.
- I don't have that information.
- I choose not to respond to an allegation of that sort. [Instead of "I don't want to answer that question."]

The "Oh My Goodness, I've Been Taken Out of Context!" Blues

Barry Greenberg, president of Celebrity Connection, was interviewed for ten hours for the *Wall Street Journal*. The sidebar quote read: "Some celebrities will go to the opening of a toilet bowl." Yes, he said it, but not "in that context."

Sometimes it is the fault of the interviewer, the producer, or the reporter, but more often it is the fault of the interviewee. If you feel you were taken out of context, the chances are you didn't attribute or qualify your remarks properly. They really quoted you as saying something that you *did* say.

If you don't want to be taken out of context, choose your words very carefully and don't make off-the-cuff comments. Don't be intimidated into saying just anything if you are not sure of the answer. Tell them you will get back to them within a certain amount of time, if you feel you must provide an answer.

If you say something, it is in context. Although your choice of words may have been inappropriate and may give the wrong impression when isolated, you still said those words and therefore you are in context.

Jack Popejoy cites this example:

"WHILE WE HAVE HAD SOME DEFICIENCIES IN OUR PRODUCTION RUN, WE'VE RECALLED ALL OF THE PRODUCTS THAT WE CAN FIND AND HAVE TAKEN STEPS TO INSURE THAT THIS NEVER HAPPENS AGAIN. WE WILL ACCEPT LIABILITY FOR ANYTHING AND EVERYTHING THAT HAS HAPPENED AS A RESULT OF THAT DEFICIENCY."

There is nothing here that can be taken out of context. But if you say this, it can be taken out of context:

"YES, SOME OF OUR PRODUCTS TURNED OUT TO BE DEFECTIVE AND SOME OF OUR CUSTOMERS WERE IN FACT HURT."

Off the Record

"Off the record" is a term that should be stricken from your speech and thinking.

People will say things *off the record* to feel as if they are wielding power with a private piece of information. Sometimes they say things *off the record* to add exclusive background to a story. Reporters who repeat the presumably sacred *off the record* information do so for the same reasons. But there is an innocent way that the information can be passed on unintentionally, and this, to me, is the most lethal. You see, once you say something, it goes into the interviewer's memory bank. But after time the *off the record* label fades away. The information remembered as innocent background in the vast storage bins of the mind.

The rule of thumb is never to tell an interviewer something *off the record*. Swallow the need to be a big shot and think of another way to tell your background information if you must. The most vulnerable time for *off the record* statements is after the interview has been completed. As Jack Popejoy warns you, "When the reporter puts down the microphone, closes the notepad, and puts the pen in the pocket, it may be that the interview is just beginning."

Corrections and Retractions

If they misspell your name, mention the wrong date, use an incorrect age, or improperly identify a photograph, then you are entitled to a correction. Asking for a correction is considered part of doing business. It gives you a serendipitous shot at coverage. You obtain a correction by calling the editorial department or sending a letter.

A retraction has to do with misquoting, misrepresentation, slander, image bashing, etc. Requesting a retraction has different implications than requesting a correction and should be well thought out before you begin the process.

To obtain a retraction, always go straight to the editor or producer—don't bother going to the interviewer. The interviewer is only a man on the game board. The editor or producer controls the game board.

To protect yourself before you do an interview, you may want to establish the retraction policy with the editor or producer. Many media people suggest that if the media can't or won't tell you the policy, then don't do business with them because they can't be trusted, and you will be the one with egg on your face, not them. This policy request should be done as politely and innocently as possible.

Even if the media has an out-in-the-open retraction policy, very few will actually do a retraction. Before I make the effort to go for a retraction, I play back the tape to hear the point in question. If it was a nuance, a lifted eyebrow, or a wink that didn't get translated into the text, wrongfully coloring what was meant, I will try for a retraction. If I get nowhere, either I or my client will write a "Letter to the Editor" or write a "Letter of Commentary" to the show, explaining our side. Publications, for the most part, although cordial, are hesitant to do retractions, offering instead to consider a "Letter to the Editor." TV or radio may offer to participate in an on-air editorial news item so your case can be told. Be careful, though, because you may open yourself up to an ongoing rebuttal dialogue. Editors don't like to lose or have you get the upper hand.

In Support of Taping Your Own Interview

If there is no video or audio proof from your side, only your word, you have no recourse if the media takes a stand against you. Being misquoted or misrepresented is a good reason why you should tape your interviews.

Jack Popejoy comments, "If I mind that you are also recording the interview as I am recording it, what could my reason possibly be? Whatever my reason for my not wanting you to record this interview is not in your best interest. If I object to your making an extemporaneous recording of the interview, then you might want to do this interview with your hat…grab it and run."

It doesn't hurt to approach the self-taping interview situation with the utmost diplomacy and courtesy. No need to make waves with those who are insecure. If you wish to avoid a conflict at the time of the interview, you could consider notifying the interviewer in ample time before the session. When I schedule the interview, I always send a confirmation letter, including the information that my client will be self-taping the interview. This gives the interviewer and the media plenty of time to digest it. Do not ask if they have a problem with this. Should you feel inclined to explain yourself, explain that it is not because you don't trust them, but you would like to study your own or your client's mannerisms and presentation. And if you do want to tell the truth, tell them that it is part of your arrangement with your lawyer, and let it rest with that. It is self-explanatory.

Taping interviews can provide you with invaluable insights and information, as well as a way to monitor technique. If you are taping your client, you can learn things that they might not have told you in your everyday conversations. Probing questions sometimes offer up interesting insights that, if cut from the story, are lost to posterity. These bits of information can be useful tools for future pitches. The more you learn about yourself or your client, the wider the corridor for more effective PR. I can't tell you the number of items for either trade or gossip columns I get from listening to the taped interview.

A *Third Person at the Interview*

Almost all media I talked with, or have had experience with, do not appreciate a third party being in the interview, even if it is a professional member of your support group. One of the skills of an interviewer is creating a rapport, a sense of intimacy used to foster trust. A good interviewer is able to open up the person they are interviewing by putting him or her at ease. Many media people felt that the third person puts a wedge between the two principals. They feel it creates a distance and doesn't allow for the intimacy that makes for a great interview. "When you have a third person," I was told, "it either cools the story or kills it."

The second most discussed reason was territorial. The interview is the interviewer's domain, not the publicist's, not the manager's, not anybody's but the interviewer's. Also stated was the feeling that with a third party present, the interviewer had backed himself or herself into a place where he or she could be criticized. Others mentioned that if there is a third party present they feel as if they should be putting on a performance or that they are being critiqued. As for refusing to do the story if there is a third party present, several said they would. The consensus of those who would still do the interview was that they would not be pleased with the situation.

Copy Approval: Can You Demand It?

A well-known saying among publicists is: "Someone else sets the type, the rest is out of our hands."

The best way to avoid having to ask for copy approval is to better equip yourself on how to be interviewed, what to say, and what not to say before you go into the interview. Don't say the wrong thing and you won't need copy approval!

Copy approval is difficult to get. I have only gotten it once in twelve years, but I do keep asking for it. I always hope for it, but deep down I recognize the right of the media to do their thing.

Los Angeles publicist Brad LeMack's opinion on copy approval brings it closer to home when he reminds us, "Of course there are pros and cons to all issues. After all, would you want Noriega to have copy approval? Then, what would you read?…he's wonderful, so he drinks a little…he's entitled, but otherwise he's a good family man? He's vacationing in Miami and he's looking forward to being home soon?" LeMack then posed the question, "Do I think the producers of *Oklahoma* should have copy approval on a review of the show?" He has a point.

Who Do You Call If the Interview Doesn't Run?

If a reporter promises that the interview will be on tonight's newscast or tomorrow's, for sure, then they know something more than their producer does. Your story can be cut by the events of the day. On May 3, 1983, KFWB Radio's Jack Popejoy told his interviewee that barring the great earthquake happening between now and then it would be on the evening news. It was about forty-five minutes later that the Coalinga, California, earthquake hit, preempting their interview. I represented the Marshall Tucker Band's New York benefit concert for WNEW-FM Radio's Christmas Fund. It was a wild and wonderful concert, but the footage never got on the air because John Lennon was killed just as they finished their last encore.

So what happens to the story? Usually the story is lost forever, especially if the event was timely. If the interview was for a developing story then the footage will go into file, and when you least expect it, there you'll be.

To track down the footage and its fate, call the assignment

desk and tell them your story. In all probability they will pass
you to the executive producer. Be inquisitive, but not pushy.

   Note: If the station is in the middle of a disaster, the same
one that preempted you, needless to say, ride out the disaster
and then call, except if the situation was timely.

12

Wrapping Up the Campaign

"I get so many kits that I can't acknowledge them. I get up to fifty calls a day asking the same questions and if I answered them all I couldn't get anything done, so don't call. *And don't ask for tear sheets!*"
—*New York Daily News*'s Liz Rittersporn's former message on her voice mail.

What's a tear sheet? In print media parlance, a tear sheet is the page(s) on which your interview, review, commentary, photo, etc., appeared in print. Why would you ask for a tear sheet? Because you might not have access to the publication. What do you do with a tear sheet once you have it? Aside from the fact that you might want to send it to your parents, the tear sheet is what makes a reprint for your media kit. If you are representing a client, a tear sheet is the proof that's in the pudding.

Many media will automatically send tear sheets because they feel it is their responsibility in exchange for the time and effort put out by the subject and the subject's support team. Unfortunately, the media who think and feel this way are few and far between. More often than not, tear sheet scavengers (a.k.a. press agents) are looked on as menacing, aggressive, insensitive, and bothersome.

The electronic media's "tear sheet" is referred to as a clip or a dub. You would think that knowing when the piece will air would be easy. It is not. If a section is backed up, the piece may be bumped to the next day or next week. If there is a disaster, the show may be preempted and programming delayed. Meanwhile you have set your VCR for 8:00 PM, Tuesday, only. And if you live in Dallas, taping a TV or radio show in Detroit is usually not feasible. So how do you get a copy? Easy, you say? Just call the segment producer and they'll send it to you? Wrong. Out of sight, out of mind, and on to the next one. Studios are not staffed nor are they equipped for duplicating services. If by chance they do agree to send you a dub, you could wait for months.

Since segment producers will discourage you from asking for a tape, and most journalists will not send you tear sheets, how do you get copies for your files and your mother? There are four methods you can follow to get your piece for your files:

1. If the media outlet is in your local area or is national, you can tape the show or buy the magazine or newspaper.
2. You can try asking the media person you dealt with to send you a tear sheet or a clip.
3. If you can determine from the journalist what date it ran, contact the publication's circulation department. Politely ask the person you are speaking with to check the column, making sure that it is the correct date. Magazines usually will not charge if you tell them it is your interview.
4. You can engage a clipping service or a video monitoring service to track the media piece.

Clipping Services

Clipping services are extremely valuable as a way of proving your worth to your client. It is very difficult and extremely time-consuming for you to personally track or follow up on every outlet. For a national mailing, it may be a full-time job. It is not only costly, but ineffective. Using a clipping service can alleviate this inconvenience. But I must place a very serious caveat emptor on this one. Clipping services are by no means 100 percent effective. I recently hired one to obtain coverage for my client, Jackie McLean, who was being honored at a Lincoln Center Tribute concert performance in New York City, and was the subject of many reviews and interviews in connection with his latest album. Not only didn't the clipping service send me the *New York Times* review of the concert, but they didn't clip the interviews and reviews in the *Boston Globe,* the *Washington Post,* or *New York Newsday!*

It is not uncommon for PR agencies to retain two clipping services simultaneously because of the many articles that slip through the cracks. This is costly, but very necessary if your business depends on the reprints to maintain the client's interest or to promote further interviews.

Clipping services clip your article and send it to you. They do this by subscribing to thousands of newspapers and magazines all over the country, employing "readers" to search for mentions of your client any way, shape, or size. The average charge is $200 a month for the print service and $1.06 a clip. Before a colleague tipped me to the secrets of the trade, I paid my share of $1.06 per clip for the most ridiculous amounts of one line listings in every Sunday TV guide across the country. What my friend told me was how to specify reading parameters. So, before you hire a clipping service, determine whether you want every mention, only stories pertaining to your client generated by interviews for which you are responsible, syndicated stories from one major market, and so on. There are countless combinations. Ask to discuss the choices, because the service may not suggest them.

In order to assist in tracking the media the services will request your media mailing list. I have yet to figure out how they miss articles when they are provided with specific media contacts. One service had difficulty finding two-column interviews in major papers, but name mentions for a TV segment came pouring in like confetti.

The print clipping services also track TV and radio, offering transcriptions (hard copy), for which they charge by the word, and video clips, for which they charge by the segment length. Giving them a specific date request is also a very good idea. There are three national clipping services that the majority of PR agencies use: Bacon's, Burrelle's, and Luce. Once again, do not empower them with your highest hopes of retrieval. Keep a checklist of mailings against clips. If you know of a specific media placement—an interview, for example, that you know appeared—you can request that they get you that paper or magazine.

Contact: Bacon's Clipping Service and Media Information Systems, 332 South Michigan Avenue, Chicago, Illinois 60604. (312) 922-2400. Outside Illinois: (800) 621-0561.

Contact: Burrelle's Clipping Service and Media Information Systems, 75 East Northfield Road, Livingston, New Jersey 07039. (800) 631-1160.

Contact: Luce Clipping Service, 420 Lexington Avenue, New York, New York 10017. (800) 628-0376.

TV Monitoring Services

If your electronic retrieval needs are not sufficient to warrant a monthly service, but you will need a pick up of only one show, or a combination of the local morning show in Detroit on Wednesday and then "Live at Five" in New York on Friday, and the "Michael Jackson Radio Show" in LA in two weeks, then you need the customized service offered by the likes of Video Monitoring Service (VMS).

VMS is the largest monitoring service of its kind, with offices in fourteen cities. VMS provides proactive and retroactive services for TV and radio broadcast news programming in 135 markets. They also selectively tape magazine-style news shows such as "60 Minutes" and "20/20." Proactive means you can order the taping ahead of time; retroactive means you can retrieve it should you have missed the air date. They do not keep the tapes past thirty days but will inform you as to archival sources.

Contact: Video Monitoring Service, 330 West 42nd Street, New York, New York 10036. (212) 736-2010.

Thank-you's

So now you have the clips in your hand, and as any nice and refined person would do, you would like to thank the person or at least acknowledge the role they have played in furthering the career of your client. Well, a pure and innocent "thank you for doing the story" can make media people very uneasy. They do not want you to perceive that they have done you a favor by doing a story. They did the story because they acted out of sound judgment and because the story was worth doing.

But if your thank-you is phrased in such a way that it appears as an acknowledgment—"I thought you really did a great job on this story," "I liked the way you captured my client's personality," or, "It was the best understanding of my client that any publication has been able to come up with"—then that goes over better. It shows them that the piece got read or seen and you took the time to consider it. Media people are supposed to be objective and not swayed by manipulation and flattery. And they are not. If anything, they resent it. And that is what they feel a thank-you means.

Thank-you's are tricky. What I usually do for print is to take the article, copy it, circle a particularly interesting line or paragraph in red grease pencil, draw a line out to the margin, and comment on how I like the way they had put this into words. For the electronic media, I usually send a note saying, "Just want you to know how much my client enjoyed doing the segment. Thanks for all your assistance in making it easy for them."

So, thank-yous are iffy, but I do them anyway, unless I learned that a particular individual is really uncomfortable getting one. I have learned to keep the message down to a dull roar, to a professional acknowledgment of their craft.

Lunch

As for wanting to thank the media in person, don't, unless they suggest it.

One of the ways that novices think is the best way to approach the subject of a thank-you is to take the person out to lunch. Well, in polite civilization it is. But this is the media—they don't have time, and they don't want to have lunch with you.

I saw a sign in an editorial office of a prominent newspaper that read:

INTERVIEWS WITH A PRESS AGENT AT LUNCH, YES.
LUNCH WITH A PRESS AGENT WITHOUT AN INTERVIEW, NO.

Enough said.

13

Don't Be Caught Unaware

"Be prepared."
—Lord Baden-Powell

This is the part that your mother, your colleagues, and your boss never prepare you for, and if I didn't, I would be just as remiss. The ways to deal with the following scenarios are probably some of the most important tools anyone could possibly give you. If you tuck them into your memory bank, they will, during the throes of PR terror, help you keep your sanity.

You have psyched out the marketplace, updated your lists, prepared a fantastic media kit, followed up on your pitch, made a date for the camera crews and the journalists to cover the event. You and/or your client are briefed on all angles of the topic, thoroughly versed in its history, statistics, and outreach. You have worked together with the segment producer or researcher and have covered the topic from your standpoint from A to Z. Both of you have agreed on a series of questions. You have practiced being interviewed. You are ready for anything, so you think. And then the media rewards you by coming to your event, and instead of covering it from the angle it was pitched, they proceed to their own agenda, often arrived at by their own research on top of your own

156

materials, leaving you "in a cloud of dust and a hearty, heigh-ho Silver."

Frank Radice, formerly executive producer of CNN and producer of "20/20," shared the inside info on this sort of agenda switch and what it means. "The crews, reporters, and journalists may choose not to go with your story pitch because nobody wants to be spoon-fed the story and the angles. The angle you provide is the one that gets them interested, but it behooves good media people to find an angle themselves; otherwise, what are they doing but re-gurgitating what you've given them? That's not original, not for them anyway. And there's an issue of ego and professional-ism that's involved. It's not a story if it's been handed to you. If you don't see it, if you don't get a glimmer of something back there in the woods that you can go after, then all you've done is become another arm for that publicist as opposed to being an arm for yourself that has the publicist working in tandem with you."

As Brian Lewis, editor of the *Los Angeles Independent*, told me, "A reporter's job is to sift through perspectives, and distill an accurate and fair account of what people need to know. This may be different from what you want them to know."

Michael Gelman, executive producer of "Live With Regis and Kathie Lee," explained, "I want to get something out of them and then I will do what they have come for. That's the way the system works. A lot of times, they don't want to give you something. They only want to come on, and give their little plug on their new product, and I say no, I don't want to do a commercial—you should buy time on the show. We're in business selling commercials for other people and making money off of it. If they want to get on my air, not as a commercial but as a segment, depending on what they are pushing, they are going to have to come to me with something for my audience, even if I have to dig it up myself."

And Gannett's Barbara Nachman hopes publicists don't get

offended or insulted by the fact that she doesn't take what we've written, copy it word for word, and put her name on it. She wants to do her own thing. "A publicist sends me a four-page media release and I might only take two sentences out of it."

What does this mean in the scheme of things? It means that you must be willing to perceive all your preparation and all the sleepless nights and creative days as an illusion—or you will go nuts. Or, as it has often been said to me, "It's not brain surgery."

With the experience of one telephone call, it will seem as if you have unlearned everything you have learned from the tips, hints, notes, and tools in this book. But what has really happened is that you are engaged in adding more to that knowledge. If you have been thwarted in your efforts, try not to view the glass as half empty. Don't go backward or escape from the awkward moments by sidestepping. Rather, stay in the moment, learn from that moment, adding it to your experience to draw from the next time you find yourself vulnerable. That is the *Zen of Hype*. No two moments are alike, therefore no recipe will work exactly the same the next time. The beauty of this is that you get to experience something new each time you create a moment. And who knows how much money or recognition that can bring you?

It is said that language precipitates the acquisition of knowledge and the expansion of behavior. I learned in speech class that Native Americans never stuttered until the white man taught them the term. So, if you can erase the word *frustration* from your vocabulary, you will not be engaged in that behavioral pattern and therefore will have a leg up when you open the newspaper to find your organization's feature article chopped to a mere paragraph about the upcoming event. Or when you tune in to the talk show and hear them present the very questions they agreed not to ask. Or when you discover that the paper had accidently printed the reporter's phone number for the registration contact number for those seven thousand potential conference participants.

Remember that media people brush their teeth the same way as everybody else. They really don't know any more than anybody else. Maybe they have become more proficient at their jobs after years of working at it, but they need our assistance to feed them, to augment them, to get them into the fray or out of a mess or over a hump. They are not the be all and end all, they are not gods, they are just mortals in a position of power, and we can be their equals through collaboration. Don't be afraid of them, don't give your power to them. Be yourself, be who you are that made you travel so far to get to the place you are—a place that has helped you obtain a coveted interview or a valuable feature story.

Don't let yourself get backed into a corner. Take the bull by the horns and show them that you have what it takes to make your media event successful.

What I am about to show you are little pieces of know-how that can make the difference between a brilliant moment and a mediocre moment. As baseball great Yogi Berra always said, "It ain't over till it's over." Here are some of the things you can do before it is over.

The bad news is that if a paper or show has a limited staff, there is no guarantee that a photographer or crew will be assigned to your event. Also, many outlets are suffering from budget cuts and don't have night or weekend crews or personnel.

The good news is that you don't have to rely on the paper's sending their own photographer to get pictures for the paper. You can hire your own photographer or video crew and submit your own pictures or tape.

It's the little things in life that make me happy, like being able to take advantage of the "limited hole and floater phenomenon." Thanks to the *New York Post*'s Marianne Goldstein, I learned of a newspaper opportunity called "a limited news hole." When they are making up the paper and there are three editorial stories with no pictures, this makes for what is called a "dry page" with plain copy. Sometimes that is the style of a paper, but where it is not, very often layout editors will try to break up the page with a photo. Often it is taken up with hard news photos. But if they don't have any hard or soft news photos for that spot, they can choose to use the photo that you submitted of your event, if it technically meets their standards. This is how a photo of a sunset or lovers holding hands or kittens gets into the paper. There is always room for what is called a "floater picture." And there is no reason why they won't use a great human interest shot from your event. So when you give instructions to your photographer to shoot the normal "grip and grin" handshake and hug shots, tell him to roam the crowd looking for a kid with ice cream on his face, or twins sleeping in the stroller amid hordes of people. It's definitely worth a try.

There are a whole series of very important questions one must be aware of in order to carry most things off. If you don't know specifically what to ask, or how to ask for information or coverage, just remember the who, what, where, when, and why that you use in every release. If you organize your questions around the 5 W's, you've got the most important bases covered.

In the case of submitting your own photographs, the most important question is: Do they use these kinds of pictures? Many papers are not "papers of record," meaning they do not report on signings, ribbon cuttings, or the usual "grip and grin" pictures that have to do with the chronicling of events (hence the term "papers of record"). In that case you're not worried because you've got the sleeping twins photo. Call the photo desk *before the event* and ask. One thing you can rely on is that they will be brutally honest.

Make sure you ask what their photo deadline is. What size photo do they want—eight by ten or three by five? Do they accept Polaroids? Do they prefer horizontal or vertical photos?

(Supplying both horizontal photos will give you a decision edge.) Do they want glossy or mat finish (nonglossy)? If the section is black and white and you only have color, will they convert them to black and white? Where and to whom should you deliver them? What entrance is open at that hour? What is the nighttime phone number to the photo desk?

Note: If the publication is in color, send color *slides*, never color prints.

When you bring them the photos, remember to identify each one with the date, event, name of the person they can call if there are questions, and the name of the photographer for photo credit should they run (use) the photo. Never write on the back with a felt tip pen or a magic marker because the type of paper used in processing is very porous. The ink will bleed (sink through) onto the front, and if you had sent two pictures without a cardboard in between, the ink from the back of the first picture will blot onto the front surface of the second picture, even though it looks dry. Write your information with pencil on a separate piece of paper and tape it to the back of the picture. Don't use regular glue, it will pucker the paper and cause a distortion on the image, rendering the photo useless.

For a photo caption (remember to include the five W's), you don't have to spend time thinking up clever or articulate copy, the newspaper has a staff who does that, and chances are they won't use your caption anyway.

It is better if you don't ask for the pictures to be returned. But if you do, specifically mark that in the information attached to the backs of the pictures. Also provide a self-addressed stamped envelope for the paper's convenience. Include a photo-sized piece of cardboard so the pictures don't get bent. But don't count on getting the pictures back. Some places may claim them as theirs, putting them in their library.

How does one find a "newspaper friendly" photographer? Photographers who are not on the newspaper's staff, but who contribute or submit their photos, are called freelancers. First, instead of looking in the yellow pages, call the photo desk and ask who they would recommend, or you can look at the photo credit which usually appears in the margin of a printed photo. Photographers are in business so they are usually listed in the yellow pages. Sometimes these are one-person operations, sometimes they belong to a photo syndicate, which means there are several photographers who shoot for a company. If the one you asked for is busy or not appropriate for your needs, they will lead you to someone else.

It is wise to make friends with these people. They make money when they sell a photo, so they know what the paper will buy and therefore what pictures to take. This is not the same as hiring a photographer for the day for your own use. A freelancer may or may not come, depending on what is scheduled for the day or whether they think they can in fact sell any picture they might take at your event. They may stay for the perfect picture and leave. This picture may not be the photo you would want to represent your event for your picture book or to give to the honoree or speaker, it will be the picture the paper would think is the best for their audience.

Freelancers will sometimes try and get you to hire them for the event. Don't let them influence you into thinking that if you don't hire them they won't come, or that if you do hire them their pictures will definitely appear in the paper. They probably didn't feel your event was worth covering in the first place and that they weren't going to be able to sell a picture, so why not get you to hire them. Don't take it personally—it is purely business.

Please, whatever you do, if your budget won't allow you to hire a photographer of worth, don't use an Instamatic camera and have your nephew develop the film with the kit he got for Christmas. Take the pictures with a 35mm camera with appropriate film. The person at the newspaper photo desk will help you, or the person at the camera shop. There is a lot riding on these photos, and you don't want to miss the opportunity.

Assigned TV crews or news crews are the most difficult to pin down, mostly because news breaks so fast. And as we learned earlier, events are preempted for hard news. Even if I have been notified that morning that they are sending a crew, I always hold my breath. But again, you do not have to be chained to the assignment desk. You don't have to rely solely on their showing up.

Send a news release to the independent video production companies the news stations hire when they don't have a crew available. Usually the independent video company will feed several stations, including cable. If they can get an assignment, or if they think they can sell the footage later, they will be there. Call the TV stations. They will tell you how to contact the independent video companies.

Traffic and weather are the other reasons for no-shows. When the assignment editor or the crew producer calls to finalize the arrangements ask them where they are coming from. If you want them there for a presentation within the event or at some particular time during the media conference, this information will guide your starting time accordingly. Figure on ample time for the crews to break down their equipment at the other site, travel time, including traffic and weather conditions, and equipment set up time at your event.

If one station commits to coming to your event, ask if they will share their footage with other stations who couldn't come. Usually they will comply because they may be in the same bind at another time. Call the other stations and alert them to who has the tape so they can access it. You do not have to get, do, or deliver anything. A problem may arise if it is a hot item. The station who shoots it may want it as an exclusive. Also, since the news is old by the next day, if the station who shot it doesn't get it edited for their use in time to give it to the other station for their processing, the best laid plans of stations and publicists often go astray.

If you get the feeling that the assignment editors are on the fence about assigning a crew, and the independent video companies are waiting to take their lead from the stations, or there are so many events that day that the possibility of the crews getting to you is one in five, hire your own news-quality video crew and submit the tapes to the news stations. There are two reasons that would make this a good idea. One is because the event means so much to you or your client that even the most remote possibility of it making it on-air is worth the expense and the effort. The other reason is if you are trying to make an impression on the invited guests, the presence of a professional crew (they don't know whose crew it is) will make your day. Be certain the person you hire knows the news deadlines and tape requirements before you hire him.

It never hurts for you to call and get a quick lesson from the news producer, so you know how to talk to the crew you intend to hire.

As for hiring freelance radio reporters, I've never heard of freelance radio reporters, unless on assignment for the station. But, hey, one never knows. Call the radio station.

Check your local newspaper daybook for conflicting events. Call the assignment editors and ask if anything is in their file for that particular day. This way you know what your competition is for priority assignments.

There is one last vestige of hope before you have to hang up your guns and vanish in the sunset to begin another release. In the best of all possible worlds, I like to schedule an event where there is no crew competition, on a weekday, early to midmorning. That way you have no competition, camera availability is assured, and the media have plenty of time to make their deadlines.

Success with such plans is possible—I have had it happen, more than once. But I often owe my success to checking in advance the calendar of events at City Hall. Anything involving politicians may automatically pull the media away from your event. Of course, a last-minute call is always possible, but if you check, at least you won't be up against the wall before you begin.

The world of hype is not very much different from any other business or any part of life. Knowing when to drop back five and kick, knowing when to fold or bluff, knowing when to wear your heart on your sleeve or when to steal away into the night are things you learn only by being in the trenches, by experiencing the day-to-day of the business. Some of us limp through, others skip through. But I've never seen anyone not smile at the thought of the circus coming to town. So, if a media person doesn't return your calls or an appearance on the morning talk show gets cut because of overtime, just think of that circus. To quote a well worn cliche, life's too short.

So take your tools, place them in your tool kit, look the world straight in the eye and pretend that thousands of happy faces and light hearts are lined up for miles as you lead the circus on its parade.

And so, the information in this book has been offered up as a tool to start you on your journey. I hope my creative tactics and concrete advice help you better understand how the process works or doesn't work, as the case may be. What I have tried to do is give you enough ammunition to cut them off at the pass, so to speak, along with the know-how to map an express route out of the pass in case you get ambushed. I have shown you the necessary basics for planning a campaign, designing a media kit, taking a useful photograph, executing a more meaningful interview, developing a stronger media presence, creating invitations that will get them there (along with the mailing lists so the invitation will get there) and how to make that all important phone call to remind them why you sent what you sent in the first place. You should have a better understanding of how to interpret the rules and play the game. And most of all, you will never be alone knowing that the library, the telephone book and directory assistance are there with almost everything you will need on your journey down the parade route.

And last but not least, my favorite tip of the trade. The biggest fear is to throw an event and have no one show up. Nobody likes an empty house, least of all the media. There is no need to give them any opportunity to comment on the attendance, or to make snide remarks on the status of the assignments. This embarrassing situation can be remedied by "padding the house"—an old vaudeville term meaning invite staff, friends, anyone who owes you a favor, or who you could stand owing you a favor.

But, most of all, remember this: If you can honestly say that you have given it everything you've got and you still don't get successful results, repeat these words: "Tomorrow is another day," "This too shall pass," and "Time heals all wounds."

Mistakes and failures are in the eyes of the beholder, but so, too, is success.

Appendix

AMERICAN BOOK TRADE DIRECTORY: BOWKER PUBLISH-ING, 121 Chanlon Road, New Providence, New Jersey 07974. (908) 665-2840.

AMERICAN PASSAGE MEDIA SERVICES, 215 West Harrison Street, Seattle, Washington 98119. (206) 282-8111.

AUDIO TV FEATURES, 149 Madison Avenue, No. 804, New York, New York 10016. (212) 889-1342.

BACON'S CLIPPING SERVICE AND MEDIA INFORMATION SYSTEMS, 332 South Michigan Avenue, Chicago, Illinois 60604. (312) 922-2400. Outside Illinois: (800) 621-0561.

BACON'S PUBLICITY CHECKERS, 332 South Michigan Avenue, Chicago, Illinois 60604. (312) 922-2400. Outside Illinois: (800) 621-0561.

BILLBOARD PUBLICATIONS, INC. (BPI): MEDIA SERVICES, 1515 Broadway, New York, New York 10036. (800) 284-4915. In New York: (212) 536-5263.

BOOK PUBLISHERS AND DISTRIBUTORS, UNITED STATES & CANADA: BOWKER PUBLISHING, 121 Chanlon Road, New Providence, New Jersey 07974. (908) 665-2840.

BOOKS IN PRINT: BOWKER PUBLISHING, 121 Chanlon Road, New Providence, New Jersey 07974. (908) 665-2840.

BOWKER PUBLISHING, 121 Chanlon Road, New Providence, New Jersey 07974. (908) 665-2840.

BROADCAST INTERVIEW SOURCE, 2233 Wisconsin Avenue N.W., No. 406, Washington, D.C. 20007-4104. (202) 333-4904.

BURRELLE'S CLIPPING SERVICE AND MEDIA INFORMATION SYSTEMS, 75 East Northfield Road, Livingston, New Jersey 07039. (800) 631-1160.

CABLE CONTACTS: BILLBOARD PUBLICATIONS, INC. (BPI), MEDIA SERVICES, 1515 Broadway, New York, New York 10036. (800) 284-4915. In New York: (212) 536-5263.

CONSULTANTS AND CONSULTING ORGANIZATIONS DIRECTORY: GALE RESEARCH, 835 Penobscot Building, Detroit, Michigan 48226. (313) 961-2242.

CONTACTS NEWSLETTER, 35-20 Broadway, Astoria, New York, 11106. (718) 721-0508.

DERUS MEDIA, 500 North Dearborn, No. 516, Chicago, Illinois 60610. (312) 644-4360.

DIRECTORY OF DIRECTORY PUBLISHERS: MORGAN-RAND DIRECTORY SERVICES, 2200 Sansom Street, Philadelphia, Pennsylvania 19103. (215) 557-8200.

DIRECTORY OF EXPERTS, AUTHORITIES AND SPOKESPERSONS: BROADCAST INTERVIEW SOURCE, 2233 Wisconsin Avenue N.W., No. 406, Washington, D.C. 20007-4104. (202) 333-4904.

DIRECTORY OF PUBLICATIONS & BROADCASTERS: GALE RESEARCH, 835 Penobscot Building, Detroit, Michigan 48226. (313) 961-2242.

DIRECTORIES IN PRINT: GALE RESEARCH, 835 Penobscot Building, Detroit, Michigan 48226. (313) 961-2242.

ENCYCLOPEDIA OF ASSOCIATIONS: GALE RESEARCH, 835 Penobscot Building, Detroit, Michigan 48226. (313) 961-2242.

FEATURE NEWS PUBLICITY OUTLETS: MORGAN-RAND DIRECTORY SERVICES, 2200 Sansom Street, Philadelphia, Pennsylvania 19103. (215) 557-8200.

GALE RESEARCH, 835 Penobscot Building, Detroit, Michigan 48226. (313) 961-2242.

THE INSIDER'S GUIDE TO BOOK EDITORS AND PUBLISHERS, St. Martin's Press, 175 Fifth Avenue, New York, New York 10010. (212) 674-5151.

LITERARY MARKETPLACE (LMP)—INTERNATIONAL LITERARY MARKETPLACE (ILMP): BOWKER PUBLISHING, 121 Chanlon Road, New Providence, New Jersey 07974. (908) 665-2840. (212) 645-9700.

LUCE CLIPPING SERVICE, 420 Lexington Avenue, New York, New York 10017. (800) 628-0376.

MEDIA DISTRIBUTION SERVICES: MDS/PRA GROUP, 1801 South Hill Street, Los Angeles, California 90015. (213) 749-7383.

METRO PUBLICITY SERVICES, 33 West 34th Street, New York, New York 10001. (212) 947-5100.

MORGAN-RAND DIRECTORY SERVICES, 2200 Sansom Street, Philadelphia, Pennsylvania 19103. (215) 557-8200.

NATIONAL FORENSIC SERVICES DIRECTORY, 17 Temple Terrace, Lawrenceville, New Jersey 08648. (609) 883-0550.

NATIONAL RADIO PUBLICITY OUTLETS: MORGAN-RAND DIRECTORY SERVICES, 2200 Sansom Street, Philadelphia, Pennsylvania 19103. (215) 557-8200.

NEWS USA INC., 2300 Clarendon Boulevard, Arlington, Virginia 22201. (800) 868-6872.

NORTH AMERICAN PRECIS SYNDICATE, INC., 4209 Vantage Avenue, Studio City, California 91604. (818) 761-8400.

PARA PUBLISHING, Mr. Dan Poynter, P.O. Box 4232, Santa Barbara, California 93103. (805) 968-7277.

PARTYLINE, 35 Sutton Place, New York, New York 10022. (212) 755-3487.

POWER MEDIA SELECTS: BROADCAST INTERVIEW SOURCE, 2233 Wisconsin Avenue, N.W., No. 406, Washington, D.C. 20007-4104. (202) 333-4904.

PR NEWSWIRE, 150 East 38th Street, New York, New York 10155. (212) 832-9400. Outside New York: (800) 832-5522.

PUBLIC RELATIONS SOCIETY OF AMERICA (PRSA), 33 Irving Place, New York, New York 10003. (212) 995-2230.

PUBLICITY EXPRESS, 1563 Solano Avenue, No. 223, Berkeley, California 94707. (800) 541-2897.

PUBLISHERS WEEKLY, 245 East 17th Street, New York, New York 10011. (212) 645-9700.

RADIO CONTACTS: BILLBOARD PUBLICATIONS, INC. (BPI), MEDIA SERVICES, 1515 Broadway, New York, New York 10036. (800) 284-4915. In New York: (212) 536-5263.

RADIO-TV REPORT: BRADLEY COMMUNICATIONS CORP., 135 East Plumstead Avenue, Landsdowne, Pennsylvania 19050. (215) 259-1070.

SPEAK AND GROW RICH, Ms. Dotty Walters, Walters Speakers Service, P.O. Box 1120, Glendora, California 91740. (818) 335-8069.

STANDARD RATE AND DATA SERVICES, 3004 Glenview Road, Wilmette, Illinois. (708) 256-6067.

SUBJECT GUIDE TO BOOKS IN PRINT: BOWKER PUBLISH-ING, 121 Chanlon Road, New Providence, New Jersey 07974. (908) 665-2840.

SYNDICATED COLUMNISTS: BILLBOARD PUBLICATIONS, INC., (BPI), MEDIA SERVICES, 1515 Broadway, New York, New York 10036. (800) 284-4915. In New York: (212) 536-5263.

TALK SHOW SELECTS: BROADCAST INTERVIEW SOURCE, 2233 Wisconsin Avenue N.W., No. 406, Washington, D.C. 20007-4104. (202) 333-4904.

TALKERS: GOODPHONE COMMUNICATIONS, INC., Box 60781, Longmeadow, Massachusetts 01116-0781. (413) 567-3189.

TV-CABLE PUBLICITY OUTLETS: MORGAN-RAND DIRECTORY SERVICES, 2200 Sansom Street, Philadelphia, Pennsylvania 19103. (215) 557-8200.

TV CONTACTS: BILLBOARD PUBLICATIONS, INC. (BPI), MEDIA SERVICES, 1515 Broadway, New York, New York 10036. (800) 284-4915. In New York: (212) 536-5263.

TV NEWS CONTACTS: BILLBOARD PUBLICATIONS, INC. (BPI), MEDIA SERVICES, 1515 Broadway, New York, New York 10036. (800) 284-4915. In New York, (212) 536-5263.

ULRICH'S INTERNATIONAL PERIODICAL DIRECTORY: BOWKER PUBLISHING, 121 Chanlon Road, New Providence, New Jersey 07974. (908) 665-2840.

VIDEO MONITORING SERVICE, 330 West 42nd Street, New York, New York 10036. (212) 736-2010.